CONTRACT ACT- SUPREME COURT'S LEADING CASE LAWS

CASE NOTES- FACTS- FINDINGS OF APEX COURT JUDGES & CITATIONS

JAYPRAKASH BANSILAL SOMANI

ISBN 979-888569838-2

Dedicated

To

All the Past & Present Judges of the Supreme Court of India.

Salute to their wisdom.

Salute to their interpretation of Law.

Salute to their elaborative judgement writing.

Contents

Contents

Preface

Dear Learned Advocates of the Trial Courts, Tribunals, High Courts, Supreme Court, & Individuals

I am very delighted to provide you a book on 'Contract Act- Supreme Court of India's Leading Case Laws'.

In this book you will get...

1. Name of the Case i. e. Cause title

2.Relevant Sections discussed in the case

3. Hon'ble Judges/Coram of the case

4.Number of PDF Pages in Original Judgement of the case

5. All available Citations of the case

6. Case Note with appeal allowed/ dismissed or disposed off

7. Facts of the case

8. Hon'ble Apex Court's findings, while dismissing/allowing or disposing the appeal

9. Ratio Decidendi if any.

My special thanks to Manupatra, because of their web portal I can compile this book in well manner. I am also thankful to Notion Press to support me to publish & market this book throughout the Country. Thanks to my Juniors, Advocate Colleagues & Insolvency Professional Colleagues to support me in this venture.

Mr Rachit Manchanda has helped me a lot to compile this book.

I hope this book will add some value addition in the wealth of your legal knowledge. Your positive feedbacks will boost me to compile/ write further books & negative feedbacks will improve my skills. Kindly send your valuable feedbacks by email.

Thanks with Regards,

Jayprakash B. Somani

Advocate, Supreme Court of India

Email: jaysomani64@gmail.com

Web Site:www.jayprakashsomani.com

Call: 8384051134, 9322188701, 9318381287

Acknowledgements

Printed & Published by
Notion Press
No. 8, 3rd Cross Street,
CIT Colony, Mylapore,
Chennai, Tamil Nadu- 600004

ᑭᑭᑭ

Managed by
Jayprakash Somani Advocates & Solicitors
Law Firm for Supreme Court of India
Delhi Office
257 C, Pocket 1, Mayur Vihar Phase 1, Delhi 110091.
Call 8384051134, 9322188701, 8459194576, 9318381287 01141051516
Supreme Court Chamber
312, 3rd Floor, M. C. Setalvad Block, In front of 'D' Gate, Bhagwan Das Road, Supreme Court of India, New Delhi 110001
Contact: 8459194576, 9811011747,
www.jayprakashsomani.com

ᑭᑭᑭ

Books are available online at
1. Notion Press: https://notionpress.com/author/jayprakash_somani
2. Amazon: https://www.amazon.in/s?k=jayprakash+somani
3. Flipkart: https://www.flipkart.com/search?q=Jayprakash%20Somani

ᑭᑭᑭ

ONE

ANDHRA SUGARS LTD. AND ORS. VS. STATE OF ANDHRA PRADESH AND ORS., 1967

Hon'ble Judges/Coram: K.N. Wanchoo, C.J., G.K. Mitter, K.S. Hegde, R.S. Bachawat and Vaidynathier Ramaswami, JJ.

Relevant Section:

Indian Contract Act, 1872 - Section 10, Section 13, Section 14, Section 15, Section 16, Section 17, Section 18, Section 19, Section 20, Section 21, Section 22, Andhra Pradesh Sugarcane (Regulation of Supply and Purchase) Act, 1961 - Section 21 Companies Act, 1956 - Section 395; Constitution Of India - Article 14, Article 286(1)(a), Article 301, Article 302, Article 304, Article 304(a), Article 32; Indian Electricity Act, 1910 [repealed] - Section 22; Sale Of Goods Act, 1930 - Section 3, Section 4, Section 4(1)

Equivalent Citation: AIR1968SC599, (1968)IMLJ117, [1968]1SCR705, [1968]21STC212(SC), MANU/SC/0245/1967

No. of pages in Original Judgement: 6

Case Note:

Other Taxes - validity of notification - Sections 2, 10, 13, 14, 15 and 22 of Indian Contract Act - sale and purchase of sugarcane exempted under State Sales Tax Act - petitioner is owner of sugar factories - State Government issued notification levying tax under Section 21 on purchase of sugar - writ under Section 32 before Supreme Court challenging validity of impugned notification - Apex Court observed contract between owner of sugar factories and suppliers of sugarcane is sale - tax to be levied on weight instead of price of goods - no discrimination is made in relation to imported cane as per Section 21 - same tax levied on all types of cane - non discriminative tax does not offend Article 301 - Section 21 (3) exempts new factories for certain period - benefit is based on legitimate legislative policy - held, notification passed by State Government is not violative of Article 14.

Brief facts of the case:

In all these writ petitions under Art. 32 of the Constitution, the petitioners ask for an order declaring that s. 21 of the Andhra Pradesh Sugarcane (Regulation of Supply and Purchase) Act, 1961 (Andhra Pradesh Act No. 45 of 1961) is unconstitutional and ultra vires and a direction prohibiting the respondents from levying tax under s. 21 and to refund the tax already collected. Section 21 of the Act is in these terms :

"21(1) The Government may, by notification, levy a tax at such rate not exceeding five rupees per metric tone as may be prescribed on the purchase of cane required for use, consumption or sale in factory.

(2) The Government may, by notification, remit in whole or in part such tax in respect of cane used or intended to be used in a factory for any purpose specified in such notification.

(3) The Government may, by notification, exempt from the payment of tax under this section -

(a) any new factory which, in the opinion of the Government has substantially expanded, to the extent of such expansion, for a period not exceeding two years from the date of completion of the expansion.

(4) The tax payable under sub-section (1) shall be levied and collected from the occupier of the factory in such manner and by such authority as may be prescribed.

(5) Arrears of tax shall carry interest at the rate of nine per cent per annum.

(6) If the tax under this section together with the interest, if any, due thereon, is not paid by the occupier of a factory within the prescribed time, it shall be recoverable from him as an arrear of land revenue."

Held,

The petitioner in Writ Petition No. 101 of 1967 raised the contention that it was a new factory and that the Government of Andhra Pradesh should have exempted it from payment of tax under s. 21(3)(a). The contention was controverted by the respondents. The affidavits do not give sufficient material on the point, nor is there any prayer in the petition for the issue of a mandamus directing the State Government to grant the exemption. In the circumstance, we do not think it fit to express any opinion on the matter. It will be open to the petitioner in Writ Petition No. 101 of 1967 to raise this contention in other proceedings.

In the result, the petitions are dismissed with costs, one hearing fee.

Petitions dismissed.

TWO

INDIAN BANK VS. K. NATARAJA PILLAI AND ORS., 1992

Hon'ble Judges/Coram: Kuldip Singh and N.M. Kasliwal, JJ.

Relevant Section:

INDIAN CONTRACT ACT, 1872 - Section 62

Equivalent Citation: 1993(1)APLJ (SC) 40, II(1995)BC299(SC), 1992 (3) CCC 342 , [1994]79CompCas674(SC), JT1992(Suppl.)S.C.1, 1993-1-LW209, 1992(2)SCALE846, (1993)1SCC493, [1992]Supp2SCR109, MANU/SC/0441/1993

No. of pages in Original Judgement: 3

Case Note:

Banking - Recovery - Appellant filed suit for recovery of an amount - High Court passed decree in favour of Appellant with interest - Hence, this Appeal - Whether, order passed by High Court was justified - Held, pronote was executed with full consideration - Defendants knowingly and with full knowledge had executed pronote - However, there was no necessity of going into question of innovation of contract as contemplated under Section 62 of the Indian Contract Act - As Defendants had executed pronote and also created equitable mortgage in favour of Bank and pronote itself contained an endorsement of "for value received" - However, there was also a statutory presumption of consideration in respect of promissory note under Section 118 of Negotiable Instruments Act, 1881 - Thus, set aside judgment and decree of High Court - Appeal allowed.

Ratio Decidendi:

"Person will be liable to pay amount if pronote is executed with full consideration."

Brief facts of the case:

The appellant - Indian Bank (in short 'the Bank') filed a suit for the recovery of an amount of Rs. 1,21,006.98 due under an equitable mortgage and pronote against three defendants, namely, K. Nataraja Pillai (defendant No. 1), his wife N. Pappathi Ammal (defendant No. 2) and his son N. Narayanan (defendant No. 3). According to the Bank, the defendant Nos. 1 to 3 executed a promissory note for Rs. 1,00,000/- on 26.8.1971 in favour of the Bank. They also executed two hypothecation deeds in respect of 'A' schedule properties and executed an equitable mortgage on 28.8.1971 for 'B' schedule properties. The consideration for the aforesaid transaction also included an amount of Rs. 71,000/- granted by the Bank in favour of 37 persons by way of short term loans. The defendant No. 1 had executed a guarantee agreement on 14.6.1971 in favour of the Bank in respect of the aforesaid short term loan in favour of 37 persons. The Bank had thus based its claim in the plaint on the promissory note and guarantee agreement for Rs. 1,00,000/- as principal and Rs. 21,006.98 as interest.

Held,

The High Court in our view has taken a wrong approach of the entire case and has ignored the important relevant documents which prove beyond any manner of doubt that the promissory note Exhibit A.1, the basis of the suit was executed with consideration and the defendant Nos. 1 and 2 were liable to pay the entire amount claimed by the Bank. Exhibit A.1 dated 26.8.1971 is the promissory note executed by the defendants in favour of the Bank for a sum of Rs. one lakh which itself recites that it was executed for 'value received'. Section 118 of the Negotiable Instruments Act, 1881 provides for a statutory presumption of consideration of every negotiable instrument which includes a promissory note. It has been established on record that all the three defendants had taken loans from the Bank and those were outstanding against them at the time of execution of the pronote. The Bank had come forward with the case in the plaint that the first defendant had obtained a medium term loan of Rs. 10,000/- on 11.9.1970 for the purpose of installing a pump set and an engine and digging a well and for which an equitable mortgage in respect of 7.86 acres of land was made in favour of the Bank. The defendant No. 1 further secured a short term loan of Rs. 2,000/- on 18.12.1970 on the security of the crops raised in his lands. The second defendant who was wife of the first defendant had obtained a short term loan of Rs. 2,000/- on 26.3.1970. The third defendant who was the son of the first defendant had also obtained a short term production loan of Rs. 2,000/- on 25.5.1971 and a further sum of Rs. 2,000/- on 15.12.1971. The defendant No. 1 had also executed a guarantee agreement on 14.6.1971 in respect of short term production loan granted to 37 persons amounting to Rs. 71,000/- . The total of the above outstandings came to Rs. 93,239.03. The defendants sought a sanction of loan for Rs. 1,00,000/- and the head office of the Bank sanctioned the said loan to the defendants on 18.8.1971 in order to cover up the earlier loans. A sum of Rs. 6,760.97 was advanced to cover up the deficiency in the sanctioned loan amount of Rs. 1,00,000/-. On 26.8.1971 the defendants executed the promissory note for the sanctioned loan amount of Rs. 1,00,000/- and to repay the amount with interest as mentioned in the pronote. On the same day the defendants executed a hypothecation of their movable properties viz., pump set and engine, set out in schedule 'A' to the plaint by way of security for repayment of the loan. They also executed another hypothecation bond in respect of the crops on the same day: On the same day, the defendants agreed to execute an equitable mortgage deed in respect of 27.02 acres of land set out in schedule 'B' of the plaint towards the loan of Rs. 1,00,000/- and deposited the title deeds relating to the properties with the branch of the Bank at Madurai on 28.8.1971. The defendants had come forward with a plea that they did not execute the aforesaid documents Exhibit A.1 and A.8 and Shri Krishnamurthy Iyer, agent of the Bank had perpetrated a fraud and that the transaction was vitiated on the ground of fraud, undue influence, coercion and misrepresentation. Both the trial court as well as the High Court found it established as a fact that the aforesaid documents were executed by the defendants knowing fully well the details of the transaction regarding the liability of Rs. 1,00,000/-. The present suit is based on the promissory note Exhibit A.1 and the equitable mortgage deeds Exhibits A.4 and A.37. Thus, so far as the question of any consideration of the guarantee agreement Exhibit A.8 is concerned, the same is of no consequence in view of the subsequent execution of the promissory note Exhibit A.1. The law enunciated in the rulings referred to above in order to hold that the guarantee agreement Exhibit A.8 dated 14.6.1971 was without consideration as the loans to 37 persons had been advanced much earlier to the execution of Exhibit A.8, will not render the promissory note to be without consideration. Now, so far as the consideration of the promissory note Exhibit A.1 is concerned, the defendants had applied for sanctioning a loan of Rs. 1,00,000/- from the Bank. The head office of the Indian Bank at Madras vide Exhibit A.127 issued a sanction order to the Indian Bank Sivaganga Branch granting a medium term loan of Rs. 1,00,000/- to the first defendant on 18.8.1971. The loan was sanctioned on the condition of obtaining joint and several demand promissory notes and an equitable mortgage deed in respect of 27.02 acres of land and hypothecation bond of 2 electric pump sets from the defendants. It further stated that the liability of a sum of Rs. 89,900/- with interest upto date should be got adjusted out of the loan of lakh of rupees. The agent of the Indian Bank Sivaganga Branch sent a communication to the first defendant on 21.8.1971 informing him of the sanction of the loan. Exhibit A.36 was the office copy of the letter whereby the first defendant had been informed of the sanction of the medium term loan of Rs. 1,00,000/ - subject to the execution of promissory note and other documents as directed by the head office. Exhibit A.37 dated 26.8.1971 is the agreement executed by the defendants in favour of the agent Indian Bank, Sivaganga Branch agreeing to create an equitable mortgage in favour of the Bank towards the loan of a lakh of rupees in respect of 27.02 acres of land. Exhibit A.38 is the registered letter sent by the first defendant to the custodian of the Indian Bank, head office, Madras intimating that the balance amount that will be paid to him after adjustment of all his liabilities, as disclosed by him under the letter marked Exhibit A.37 may not be sufficient for him to carry on his agricultural operations and as such requesting to sanction a medium short term loan of not less that Rs. 20,000/- and also requested to direct the agent Indian Bank, Sivaganga Branch to return the promissory notes and other connected documents to enable him to collect the amounts from the concerned parties. Apart from the aforesaid documents, Exhibit A.39 is the office copy of the letter sent by the agent Indian Bank, Sivaganga Branch to the first defendant asking him to take delivery of the promissory notes relating to 37 persons after passing a receipt for the same on 13.9.1972. It may be further noted that out of the amount of Rs. 6,760.97 credited in the account of defendants, a sum of Rs. 6,200/- was withdrawn by the first defendant on 7.10.1971 through Exhibit A.52, a cheque drawn in favour of self. This proves beyond any manner of doubt that the defendants had accepted the sanctioning of loan of Rs. 1,00,000/- on the terms and conditions laid down by the head office of the Bank and as such sanctioning of loan clearly contained the adjustment of the liability of the 37 persons. Exhibit A.126 is a true copy of the loan amount of the defendants as per ledger folio 4/168 of the Indian Bank, Sivaganga Branch, which shows a liability of Rs. 1,21,006.98. The trial court had relied on all the aforesaid documents and had recorded a finding that the suit promissory note was fully supported by consideration and the equitable mortgage deed created by the defendants were also true and valid documents. The High Court, in our view was wrong in arriving at the conclusion that Exhibit A.1 failed for want of consideration to the extent of Rs. 74,190.56 and also for the amount advanced to the third defendant, the liability in respect of which came to Rs. 4,193.19.

We agree with the finding of the trial court that the pronote Exhibit A.1 dated 26.8.1971 was executed with full consideration. The defendants knowingly and with full knowledge had executed the pronote Exhibit A.1. In the facts and circumstances of the case, there was no necessity of going into the question of novation of contract as contemplated under Section 62 of the Indian Contract Act. The defendants had executed the pronote and also created equitable mortgage in favour of the Bank and the pronote itself contained an endorsement of "for value received". As already mentioned above, there is also a statutory presumption of consideration in respect of the promissory note under Section 118 of the Negotiable Instruments Act, 1881. In these circumstances, we allow this appeal, set aside the judgment and decree passed by the High Court and restore the judgment and decree of the trial court with costs.

THREE

RAMAGYA PRASAD GUPTA AND ORS. VS. MURLI PRASAD AND ORS., 1974

Hon'ble Judges/Coram: H.R. Khanna, P. Jaganmohan Reddy and P.K. Goswami, JJ.

Relevant Section:

INDIAN CONTRACT ACT, 1872 - Section 65; CODE OF CIVIL PROCEDURE, 1908 (CPC) - Section 11

Equivalent Citation: AIR1974SC1320, 1974()PLJR441, 1974(7)PLJR441, (1974)2SCC266, [1974]3SCR915, 1974(6)UJ574, MANU/SC/0018/1974

No. of pages in Original Judgement: 7

Case Note:

Civil - right of compensation - Section 11 of CPC, 1908, Section 9 (2) and 9 (3) of Indian Electricity Act, 1910, Sections 24, 65 and 70 of Indian Contract Act, 1872, Sections 39 and 41 of Specific Relief Act, 1963, Section 144 of Criminal Procedure Code, 1973 and Section 14 of Partnership Act - judgment of High Court challenged - respondent entered into an oral agreement of partnership with four other person and purchased electrical undertaking - later partnership dissolved license got cancelled and firm declared illegal and void - whether respondent-plaintiff was solely entitled to compensation from State Government - Apex Court observed that if knowledge is an essential requisite even an agreement ab initio void can be discovered to be void subsequently - there may be cases where parties enter into an agreement thinking that it is as perfectly legal agreement and one of them sues other or wants other to act on it then he may discover it to be void - agreement of partnership was entered between respondent and failure of appellant before purchasing electric licence - held, respondent not entitled solely to whole of compensation money all those whose names appear in partnership deed or legal representatives or assignees of such partners are entitled to share in compensation.

Brief facts of the case:

These appeals are by certificate against the judgment of the Patna High Court which reversed the judgment and decree of the Trial Court in Title Suit No. 94 of 1956 filed by the first respondent Murli Prasad. A brief history of this case will be necessary for understanding the several contentions urged before us. One Mahendra prasad obtained a licence for electrification of the Chhapra town which was granted to biro in 1932. The licence was thereafter assigned to Janardhan Prasad Varma after the death of his father Mahendra Prasad in 1936. This licence was subsequently assigned to the Cnhapra Electric Supply Co., Ltd., which, however, went into voluntary liquidation in 1944. It was decided to sell the electricity undertaking by public auction and assign the licence to the purchaser with the previous sanction of the Government, In pursuance of this decision, the liquidator invited bidders for purchasing the electricity concern. But before the date of public auction, it is alleged that five persons, namely, Ayodhya Prasad, Murli Prasad Respondent No. 1, Parasnath Prasad, Gurbharan Shah and Nandkishore Prasad entered into an oral agreement of partnership to purchase the electrical undertaking in the name of Murli Prasad, the share of Ayodhya was 8 annas, that of Murli Prasad 4 annas, Parasnath Prasad had 2 annas and Gurbharan Shah and Nandkishore Prasad had one anna each. It was also agreed that the licence will be obtained in the name of Murli Prasad alone, though each partner had to contribute to the total purchase money in proportion of their respective shares in the partnership. Thereafter the electrical undertaking was sold by the official liquidator on September 15,1944 to Murli Prasad as his was the highest bid of Rs. 4,10,000/-. Thereafter each of the partners including Murli Prasad contributed in proportion to their respective shares in the partnership to make up the total sum of Rs. 4,10,000/-. Payments to the official liquidator were made in three installments. It also appears that before the last installment of Rs. 2,50,000/- was paid on July 13, 1945, the oral agreement entered into between the partners was incorporated into a partnership deed executed on July 10, 1945 and registered under the Indian Registration Act: (Exhibit 'G'). Each of the partners had paid the following sums in accordance with their respective shares and in this manner all of them contributed Rs. 4,10,000/-towards the purchase money paid to the liquidator: Ajodhya Prasad Gupta-Rs. 2,05,000/-; Murli Priisad-Rs. 1,02,500/-; Parasnath Prasad-Rs. 51,250/-; Gurbharan Shah Rs. 25,625/-and Nandkishore Prasad-Rs. 25,625/-. Nandkishore Prasad, however, retired from the partnership with the consent of all the partners and his one anna share was taken over by Gurbharan Shah. It also appears that in 1950 a further sum of Rs. 1,50,0007-was urgently required for taking delivery of some new plant and machinery which had arrived at the Chhapra Railway Station. Murli Prasad and Parasnath Prasad expressed their inability to contribute the sum of Rs. 1,50,000/-in proportion to their shares, so this amount was also paid by Ajodhya Prasad Gupta to whom Murli Prasad and Parasnath Prasad sold one anna share each out of their respective shares. Thus, the share of Ajodhva Prasad increased to 10 annas while that of Murli Prasad and Parasnath Prasrd reduced to 3 annas and one anna respectively. Thereafter the partners contributed the amount in accordance with their respective shares. This re-allocation of shares became the occasion for execution of a second partnership deed on August 31. 1950 which was also registered under the Indian Registration Act: Ext. 9. The partnership Act on May 13, 1953, Ext. 'C'. One other fact must also be stated at this stage, and that is, Ayodhya Prasad and Murli Prasad being Kartas of the respective joint families, had entered into partnership in that capacity. The 10 annas share held by Ajodhya Prasad and 3 annas share held by Murli Prasad were divided among the members of their respective joint families. The share of Murli Prasad was divided between himself, Dharmdhar Prasad each having one anna share, while the sons of Murli Prasad and Dharmdhar Prasad, namely, Chandreshwar Prasad Gupta and Kamleshwar Prasad Gupta and each 6 pies share. Similarly, Ajodhya Prasad's and his brother Ram Sharan Shah got 3 annas 9 pies each while the two sons of Ram Sharan Shah, Brahmadev Prasad Gupta and Ramagya Prasad Gupta and respectively 1 anna 3 pies. There was no change in the shares of the two remaining partners Parasnath Prasad and Gurbharan Shah who held one anna and two annas share respectively.

Held,

In our opinion, the view of the learned authors is neither supported by any of the subsequent Privy Council decisions nor is it consistent with the natural meaning to be given to the provisions of Section 65. The section by using the words 'when an agreement is discovered to be void' means nothing more nor less than : when the plaintiff comes to know or finds nut that the agreement is void. The word 'discovery' would imply the ore-existence of something which subsequently found out and it may be observed that Section 66, Hyderabad Contract Act makes the knowledge film of the agreement been void as one of the pre-requisites for restitution and is used in the sense of an agreement being discovered to be void. If knowledge is an essential requisite even an agreement at initio void can be discovered to be void subsequently. There may be cases where parties enter into an agreement honestly "thinking that it is a perfectly legal agreement and where one of them sues the other or wants the other to act on it, it is then that he may discover it to be void. There is nothing specific in Section 65. Indian Contract Act or its corresponding section of the Hyderabad Contract Act to make it inapplicable to the such cases.

The above view, which has been noticed in subsequent edition of Pollock's Book (See 9th Edition, p. 463 Note 41), is in consonance with authority, equity and good reason. After this conclusion it is not necessary to consider whether Section 70 of the Contract Act or Section 39 and 41 of the Specific Relief Act can be invoked in aid of the appellants.

On any view of the matter whether the agreement was void at initio, or was void or valid initially but became void or discovered to be void subsequently, the appellants are entitled to succeed in these appeals. We accordingly allow these appeals, reverse the judgment and decree of the High Court and dismiss Suit No. 94 of 1956 with costs. We hold that the first respondent Murli Prasad is not entitled solely to the whole of the compensation money, but that all those whose names appear in the partnership deed of August 31, 1950, or the legal representatives or assignees of such of them who are dead, are otherwise entitled to share the compensation money in proportion to their respective shares as specified in the said document. The compensation amount which is so distributed is the balance of the amount remaining after payment of the outstanding liabilities of the Chhapra Electric Supply Works. The Trial Court will give the necessary directions to the Receiver in this behalf

PPP

FOUR

HARI CHAND MADAN GOPAL AND ORS. VS. STATE OF PUNJAB

Hon'ble Judges/Coram: D.G. Palekar, J.M. Shelat, K.K. Mathew, S.N. Dwivedi and Y.V. Chandrachud, JJ.

Relevant Section:

Indian Contract Act, 1872 - Section 63, GOVERNMENT OF INDIA ACT, 1833 [REPEALED] - Section 175,Section 107, Section 175, Section 175(3), Section 177(1), Section 179(1);

Equivalent Citation: AIR1973SC381, (1973)1SCC204, [1973]2SCR582, MANU/SC/0021/1972

No. of pages in Original Judgement: 27

Case Note:

Commercial - remission - Section 63 of Indian Contract Act, Punjab Partition (Contracts) Order, 1947 and Section 9 (2) of Indian Independence Act, 1947 - appellants owed money to Government being clearing agent of former - Government's claim of recovery of money resisted on ground of arbitral award - money originally owed to undivided Punjab - on independence arbitrator appointed to decide liabilities of East and West Punjab on partition - Government of West Punjab entitled for 40% of claims of undivided Punjab as per arbitral award - Government cannot claim more than 40% on ground that they paid to sellers of agricultural produces to appellants as such payment was without consent of appellant.

Brief facts of the case:

The factual framework of this appeal is set spastically in the undivided geography of India during the British period and temporarily during 1944 to June 1947. There are three appellants:

Messrs Hari Chand Madan Gopal and Co., (2) Hari Chand and (3) Sri Ram. The first appellant is a partnership firm, of which the other two appellants are partners. Some time in 1944 there was concluded an agreement between the first appellant and the Government of the Province of Punjab (hereinafter called the Undivided Punjab). By that agreement, the first appellant agreed to act as a Clearing Agent (Foodgrains) for the sale and purchase of foodgrains on behalf of the Undivided Punjab on payment of a commission. The first appellant obtained stock of rice from the Rationing Controllers of the districts which were after the Partition of India in August 1947 included in the State of East Punjab and are now included in the State of Punjab. According to the State of Punjab (the plaintiff-respondent) the price of the stock supplied by the said Rationing Controllers was Rs. 12,15,178/4/11. The stock was supplied in May and June, 1947. The first appellant sold the said stock to persons in Delhi and the United Provinces (now called Uttar Pradesh). The plaint admits the receipt of three amounts : (1) a sum of Rs. 2,91.817/13/11/2 , (2) a sum of Rs. 2,67,963/10/1, collected from various purchasers in Delhi and Uttar Pradesh to whom the first appellant had sold the stock, and (3) a sum of Rs. 20,000/-paid by the first appellant. The aggregate of receipts thus comes to Rs. 5,79,841/8/1/2. Deducting the aggregate amount from the total sum due, there still remains an outstanding of Rs. 6,03,897/-/9. It is alleged in paragraph 9 of the plaint that on July 29, 1953. the appellants admitted their liability to pay the said amount.The third appellant did not enter appearance. The case proceeded ex-parte against him in the trial court.

Held,

This inference is supported by the subsequent conduct of the Government Officers. After January 17, 1951, the Government had sent letters to the appellants indicating that payment to sellers was an essential term of the proposed settlement of January 17, 1951. A similar letter was never sent to the appellant after July 28-29, 1953. On the other hand, letters of the Director, Food and Civil Supplies, dated April 21, 1954 and May 11, 1954 show that the Government was paying the sellers from the amount with it to the credit of the appellants and asking them to give their consent to such payment. The Director, Food and Civil Supplies, sent five letters to the appellants on April 21, 1954. They are exhibits D-6 to D-11. In each of them he has stated that if no reply were received within a fortnight, it would be presumed that the appellants had agreed to the payment being made to the sellers mentioned in the letters. The appellants replied to those five letters on May 3, 1954. They said that unless a detailed account of their post-partition dealings was made available to them, it would not be possible to reply to the Director's letters. The Director was requested to send a complete copy of the accounts. In his reply letter of May 11, 1954, the Director said that the appellants had already been given details of the accounts in the meeting of July 28 and 29, 1953. He concluded by saying that if no reply was received by him up to May 20, 1954, it would be presumed that they had no objection to the payment being made to the sellers and that "this office would proceed to make payment to the parties concerned." These letters indicate that in spite of the absence of consent by the appellants, the Government was paying sellers from the amount with it to the credit of the appellants. These letters show that instead of insisting upon payment to the sellers by the appellants, the Government was accepting and acting according to the appellants' proposal of January 17, 1951 that the sellers should be paid by the Government from the money with it to the credit of the appellants.

In view of the foregoing discussion, we are of the view, that the Government had decided to recover only 40% and no more. The Government's decision would amount to remitting a part of the debt due by the appellants. Under Section 63 of the Contract Act. a promise can remit a promise in part. It is not necessary under the Contract Act that such remission should be supported by consideration. If the decision of the Government amounts to remitting a part of the debt, as we think, then the Government cannot seek to recover more than 40%. Admittedly more than 40% of the total liability has already been paid to the Government. Therefore nothing remains due by the appellants.

Accordingly we allow the appeal and dismiss the suit of the Government. In the peculiar circumstances of this case, the appellants shall get no costs throughout.

ÞÞÞ

FIVE

Assistant General Manager and Ors. Vs. Radhey Shyam Pandey, 2020

Hon'ble Judges/Coram: Arun Mishra, M.R. Shah and B.R. Gavai, JJ.

Acts/Rules/Orders:

Provident Fund Rules; Banking Companies (Acquisition and Transfer of Undertakings) Act, 1970; Bombay Agricultural Produce Markets Act, 1939 - Section 26, Section 26(1), Section 26(5); Constitution of India - Article 12, Article 14, Article 15, Article 16, Article 16(1), Article 19, Article 19(1), Article 21, Article 311, Article 311(2); Consumer Credit Act; Fair Trading Act, 1973; Finance Act, 2000; German Civil Code - Section 138(2); Gujarat Agricultural Produce Markets Act, 1963 - Section 64; Income-tax Act, 1961 - Section 10(10C); Indian Contract Act, 1872 - Section 16(1), Section 16(2), Section 17, Section 19, Section 19A, Section 23, Section 24, Section 29(5), Section 208; Payment of Gratuity Act, 1972; Punjab National Bank (Employees) Pension Regulations, 1995 - Regulation 2, Punjab National Bank (Employees) Pension Regulations, 1995 - Regulation 9(b), Punjab National Bank (Employees) Pension Regulations, 1995 - Regulation 28, Punjab National Bank (Employees) Pension Regulations, 1995 - Regulation 29, Punjab National Bank (Employees) Pension Regulations, 1995 - Regulation 29(1), Punjab National Bank (Employees) Pension Regulations, 1995 - Regulation 29(4), Regulation 29(5), Regulation 30, Punjab National Bank (Employees) Pension

Regulations, 1995 - Regulation 31, Punjab National Bank (Employees) Pension Regulations, 1995 - Regulation 32, Punjab National Bank (Employees) Pension Regulations, 1995 - Regulation 33, Punjab National Bank (Employees) Pension Regulations, 1995 - Regulation 34; Restrictive Trade Practices Act, 1956; State Bank Of India Act, 1955 - Section 49, State Bank Of India Act, 1955 - Section 50, State Bank Of India Act, 1955 - Section 50(1), State Bank Of India Act, 1955 - Section 50(2); State Bank of India Employees Pension Fund Rules - Rule 8, State Bank of India Employees Pension Fund Rules - Rule 2BA, State Bank of India Employees Pension Fund Rules - Rule 22, State Bank of India Employees Pension Fund Rules - Rule 22(iii), State Bank of India Employees Pension Fund Rules - Rule 22(i), State Bank of India Employees Pension Fund Rules - Rule 23, State Bank of India Employees Pension Fund Rules - Rule 148(3), State Bank of India Employees Pension Fund Rules - Rule 149(3); Supply of Goods (Implied Terms) Act; Unfair Contract Terms Act, 1977

Equivalent Citation: 2020(8)ADJ179, 2020 6 AWC5782SC, 2021(1)BLJ73, 2020(II)CLR51, 2021(1)ESC299(SC), (2020)6SCC438, (2020)2SCC(LS)523, 2020 (5) SCJ 347, 2020(2)SCT305(SC), 2020(5)SLR282(SC), MANU/SC/0252/2020

No. of pages in Original Judgement: 27

Case Note:

Service - Pension - Voluntarily retirement scheme - After obtaining approval of Government of India, Indian Bank Association (IBA) evolved Voluntary Retirement Scheme (VRS) - Central Board of Directors of Bank adopted and approved scheme in its meeting for implementing VRS for employees of bank by retiring them on completion of fifteen years of service with benefit provided in scheme - After Central Board of SBI approved proposals, circular was issued which made it clear that gratuity, provident fund contribution as per the Provident Fund Rules, pension in terms of SBI Employees' Pension Fund Rules, leave encashment to be provided beside amount of ex gratia- Respondent questioned refusal of bank to pay pension in writ application filed in High Court - Respondent retired and bank accepted offer of employee to retire him voluntarily - High Court held that case of employee fell under Second Part of Rule 22(i)(a) of Rules and admissible benefit could not be denied - Hence, present appeal - Whether Respondent-employees were entitled to pension on completion of fifteen years of service as per State Bank of India Voluntary Retirement Scheme.

Brief facts of the case:

After obtaining approval of the Government of India, the Indian Bank Association (IBA) evolved a Voluntary Retirement Scheme. The Central Board of Directors of the State Bank of India (SBI) adopted and approved the scheme in its meeting for implementing the VRS for the employees of the bank by retiring them on completion of fifteen years of service with the benefit provided in the scheme. The scheme had been drawn up, keeping in view the guidelines issued by the IBA. After the Central Board of SBI approved the proposals contained in the memorandum, a circular was issued in which it was mentioned that the IBA advised that as the Committee constituted by the Finance Ministry recommended introduction of a VRS in order to rationalise the manpower, the Government of India had no objection for adopting and implementing the VRS. It was clearly stated in the Circular that the Central Board of Directors accorded approval for adopting and implementing the SBI voluntary Retirement Scheme drawn up, keeping in view the guidelines issued by the IBA. The circular also made it clear that gratuity, provident fund contribution as per the Provident Fund Rules, pension in terms of the SBI Employees' Pension Fund Rules, leave encashment to be provided beside the amount of ex gratia. Respondent questioned the refusal of the bank to pay pension in the writ application filed in the High Court. He retired under the SBI VRS. The bank accepted the offer of the employee to retire him voluntarily. He was aged fifteen years three months and had nine months service still to go before attaining the age of superannuation. When the VRS became effective, he had put in nineteen years, nine months, and eighteen days of pensionable service. He had to retire on completion of sixty years, and would have put in a little more than twenty years of pensionable service. The High Court held that the case of the employee fell under the Second Part of Rule 22(i)(a). He was in service of the bank and completed ten years of pensionable service, and further, he attained the age of fifty eight years before the date he retired. The High Court opined that the clarification was not part of the VRS scheme. The employee retired outside Rule as per the contractual retirement scheme. The contract had to prevail. In Pension Fund Rules, Clause (a) in Rule 22(i) was inserted to give the employees the benefit of pension after ten years of pensionable service even if they had joined late. The High Court found that the matter was covered by Rule 22(i)(a). The admissible benefit could not be denied. If a contracting party is entitled to take benefit of a permissible clause, then it could not be denied to him.

Held,

This Court observed that the principal aim of the socialist State as envisaged in the Preamble is to eliminate inequality. The basic framework of socialism is to provide security in the fall of life to the working people and especially provides security from the cradle to the grave when employees have rendered service in heydays of life, they cannot be destituted in old age, by taking action in an arbitrary manner and for omission to complete obligation assured one. Though there cannot be estoppel against the law but when a bank had the power to amend it, it cannot take shelter of its own inaction and SBI ought to have followed the pursuit of other banks and was required to act in a similar fair manner having accepted the scheme.

Resultantly, we are of the opinion that the employees who completed 15 years of service or more as on cut-off date were entitled to proportionate pension under SBI VRS to be computed as per SBI Pension Fund Rules. Let the benefits be extended to all such similar employees retired under VRS on completion of 15 years of service without requiring them to rush to the court. However, considering the facts and circumstances, it would not be appropriate to burden the bank with interest. Let order be complied with and arrears be paid within three months, failing which amount to carry interest at the rate of 6 per cent per annum from the date of this order. The appeals are accordingly disposed of. No costs.

SIX

BRITISH INDIA STEAM NAVIGATION CO. LTD. VS. SHANMUGHAVILAS CASHEW INDUSTRIES AND ORS., 1990

Hon'ble Judges/Coram: K.N. Saikia and P.B. Sawant, JJ.

Relevant Section:

INDIAN CONTRACT ACT, 1872 - Section 28

Equivalent Citation: 1990 (2) CCC 159 , (1990)2CompLJ1(SC), (1990)2CompLJ1(SC), 1990(48)ELT481(S.C.), JT1990(1)SC528, 1990(1)SCALE462, (1990)3SCC481, [1990]1SCR884a, 1990(2)UJ47, MANU/SC/0467/1990

No. of pages in Original Judgement: 8

Case Note:

Contract - Claim of - Indian Carriage of Goods by Sea Act, 1925 - Whether appellant would be liable for suit claim in lieu of shortage of delivery? - Held, it can not be said that shipper, whose knowledge will be attributed to first respondent did not know of conditions of carriage printed on reverse there being no other conditions printed elsewhere in the bills of lading - Unless starting point or port of loading is a port in India Rules are inapplicable - Rules have no application when goods are not carried from any Indian port - As in case goods were shipped in Africa and carried to Cochin, Act,1925 was not applicable - There is nothing to show that charterparty was by way of demise and Pacta dant legem contractui stipulations of parties constitute law of contract - Agreements give law to contract - Appeal allowed

Brief facts of the case:

The first respondent M/s. Shanmughavilas Cashew Industries, Quilon purchased from East Africa 350 tons of raw cashew nuts which were shipped in the vessel SS Steliosm chartered by the appellant M/s. British India Steam Navigation Co. Ltd., incorporated in England, pursuant to a contract of affreightment evidenced by 3 bills of lading issued to the shipper for the 3 loads of cashewnuts. Out of 4445 bags containing the nuts carried in the said vessel only 3712 bags were delivered at Cochin, there being thus short landing of 733 bags.

The first respondent sued the appellant in suit No. O.S. 18/1965 in the Court of the Subordinate Judge, Cochin seeking damages for the shortage of 733 bags of raw cashewnuts amounting to Rs.44,438.03. The suit having been decreed with interest @ 6% per annum from 17.7.1964, for the sum total of Rs.46,659.93, the appellant preferred therefrom appeal A.S. No. 365 of 1969 in the High Court of Kerala which was pleased by its Judgments and decree dated 16.8.1973 and 30.11.1973, to dismiss the appeal and affirm that of the Subordinate Judge. Aggrieved, the appellant has preferred this appeal by special leave.

Held,

There is nothing to show that the charterparty was by way of demise. Pacta dant legem contractui the stipulations of parties constitute the law of the contract. Agreements give the law to the contract. Clause 4 having been a stipulation in the contract evidenced by the bills of lading the parties could not resile therefrom. It is not clear whether the English Carriage of Goods by Sea Act, 1924 or the Indian Carriage of Goods Act, 1925 was applied by the High Court. The Articles and the Rules referred to are to be found in the Schedule to the Indian Act the Rules whereunder were not applicable to the facts of the case. The dispute could not have been decided partly according to municipal law and partly according to English law. The English law was not proved before the court according to law.

The result is that this appeal must succeed. We accordingly allow this appeal, set aside the impugned judgments and remand the case to the trial court for disposal according to law after giving opportunity to the parties to amend their pleadings and adduce additional evidence, if they are so advised, in light of the observations made hereinabove. In the facts and circumstances of the case we make no order as to costs.

ÞÞÞ

SEVEN

K.P. CHOWDHARY VS. STATE OF MADHYA PRADESH AND ORS., 1996

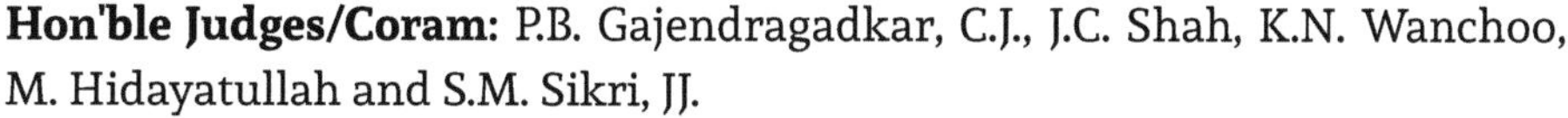

Hon'ble Judges/Coram: P.B. Gajendragadkar, C.J., J.C. Shah, K.N. Wanchoo, M. Hidayatullah and S.M. Sikri, JJ.

Relevant Section:

CONSTITUTION OF INDIA - Article 299(1); GOVERNMENT OF INDIA ACT, 1935 [REPEALED] - Section 175(3) Constitution Of India - Article 299, Article 299(1); Government Of India Act, 1935 [repealed] - Section 175, Section 175(3); Indian Contract Act, 1872 - Section 70; Indian Forest Act, 1927 - Section 82, Section 85

Equivalent Citation: AIR1967SC203, 1966JLJ1012(SC), 1966MhLJ988, 1966MPLJ1057, [1966]3SCR919, MANU/SC/0023/1966

No. of pages in Original Judgement: 3

Case Note:

Commercial - arrears of land revenue - Sections 82 and 85 of Indian Forest Act, 1927, Rules 28 and 29 of Madhya Pradesh Forest Contract Rules, Articles 299 and 299 (1) of Constitution of India, Section 155 of Madhya Pradesh Land Revenue Code, 1959, Section 175 (3) of Government of India Act, 1935 and Section 70 of Indian Contract Act, 1872 - questions arising in this appeal is whether Article 299 hits an implied contract and amount due can be recovered as arrears of land revenue under Section 155 (b) or some other provisions of law - under Article 299 (1) there can be no implied contracts between Government and any other party as State cannot be saddled with liability for unauthorized contracts - in absence of any contract executed according to terms of Article 299 (1) no money can be recovered by State as arrears of land revenue under Section 155 (b) - held, case is remanded back to High Court to decide possibility of recovering amount from appellant under any other provision of law

Brief facts of the case:

This is an appeal by special leave against the judgment of the Madhya Pradesh High Court. The brief facts necessary for present purposes are these. A notice was issued by the Divisional Forest Officer, Jabalpur Division for auction of various contracts in that division in July 1959. The conditions of the auction specified inter alia (a) that no person would be allowed to bid for any forest contract at the auction unless he had signed the sale notice in token of his agreement to abide by the conditions thereof and deposited a sum of Rs. 500/- as earnest money in respect of each forest contract before bidding therefore; (b) that the Divisional Forest Officer reserved to himself the power without assigning any reason to accept the highest or any bid, (c) that the consideration due under a contract was to be payable where it exceeded Rs. 3,000/-, in four equal installments, the first installment being payable immediately at the close of the auction; (d) that the successful bidder had to sign immediately at the close of the auction the bid-sheet for the contract knocked down in his favour; (e) that the sales of contracts beyond the power of sanction of the Divisional Forest Officer were subject to the sanction of the competent authority and the successful bidder was bound by his bid until orders were passed by the competent authority; (f) that the contract deed and the security bond were to be executed by the successful bidder and his surety immediately at the close of the auction; (g) that if the successful bidder fails to pay the full amount of the consideration, or the first installment or to furnish the security required or to complete the formalities, the earnest money deposited by him was to be forfeited to Government and the contract would be re-auctioned at the risk of the successful bidder and any deficiency happening on such re-sale would be recoverable from the successful bidder as arrears of land revenue; and (h) that the act of bidding was deemed to be a complete and unreserved acceptance of these conditions and others which are not material for our purposes.

Held,

What was said in these cases with respect to s. 175(3) of the Government of India Act, 1935, applies with equal force to Art. 299(1) of the Constitution. Two consequences follow from these decisions. The first is that in view of Art. 299(1) there can be no implied contract between the Government and another person, the reason being that if such implied contracts between the Government and another person were allowed, they would in effect make Art. 299(1) useless, for then a person who had a contract with Government which was not executed at all in the manner provided in Art. 299(1) could get away by saying that an implied contract may be inferred on the facts and circumstances of a particular case. This is of course not to say that if there is a valid contract as envisaged by Art. 299(1), there may not be implications arising out of such a contract. The second consequence which follows from these decisions is that if the contract between Government and another person is not in full compliance with Art. 299(1) it would be no contract at all and could not be enforced either by the Government or by the other person as a contract. In the present case it is not in dispute that there never was a contract as required by Art. 299(1) of the Constitution. Nor can the fact that the appellant bid at the auction and signed the bid-sheet at the close thereof or signed the declaration necessary before he could bid at the auction amount to a contract between him and the Government satisfying all the conditions of Art. 299(1). The position therefore is that there was no contract between the appellant and the Government before he bid at the auction, nor was there any contract between him and the Government after the auction was over as required by Art. 299(1) of the Constitution. Further, in view of the mandatory terms of Art. 299(1), no implied contract could be spelled out between the Government and the appellant at the stage of bidding for Art 299 in effect rules out all implied contracts between Government and another person. The view taken by the High Court that s. 155(b) of the Madhya Pradesh Land Revenue Code which provides for recovery of money as arrears of land revenue would therefore enure in favour of the Government and enable it to recover the deficiency cannot be sustained. That clause provides for recovery of all moneys falling due to the State Government under any grant, lease or contract and says that they shall be recoverable in the same manner as arrears of land revenue. The High Court was of the view that the word "contract" in this clause includes an implied contract. But if there can be no implied contract between the Government and another person in view of the mandatory provision of Art. 299(1) of the Constitution there can be no question of recovery of any money under an implied contract under Clause (b) of s. 155. The view therefore taken by the High Court that this amount could be recovered under s. 155(b) is not correct.

This brings us to the second question, namely, whether the amount can be recovered under any other provision of law as arrears of land revenue. In this connection learned counsel for the State has referred us to s. 82 and s. 85 of the Indian Forest Act. The question whether the amount can be recovered either under s. 82 or under s. 85 of the Indian Forest Act read with the rules framed thereunder has not been investigated by the High Court. The view of the High Court that Rules 28 and 29 of the Forest Contract Rules apply after a contract in writing has been executed appears to be correct. But the question whether the State can still recover the amount as arrears of land revenue by virtue of the conditions of auction, even though Rules 28 and 29 do not apply has not been investigated. This question will require investigation before the petition can be finally disposed of. The appellant had claimed in para 17 of the petition that the claim of the State for recovery of the deficiency on re-sale was not covered under any other provision of law so as to make it recoverable as arrears of land revenue. That question has still to be investigated and it would be for the State to show whether the amount can be recovered under any provision of law or rules relating to forest contracts. So the matter will have to be remanded for further investigation on these lines.

We therefore allow the appeal and hold that s. 155(b) of the Madhya Pradesh Land Revenue Code does not assist the state in realising this amount as arrears of land revenue. We however remand the matter to the High Court for determining after hearing both parties whether there is any other provision of law or rules which would permit the recovery of this amount in view of the conditions of auction. In the circumstances we order parties to bear their own costs of this Court.

Appeal allowed.

EIGHT

MAHANAGAR TELEPHONE NIGAM LTD. VS. TATA COMMUNICATIONS LTD., 2019

Hon'ble Judges/Coram: Rohinton Fali Nariman and Vineet Saran, JJ.

Relevant Section:

Indian Contract Act, 1872 - Section 74; Section 73; Section 70

Equivalent Citation: AIR2019SC1233, 2019(2)ALT196, 2020 (3) CCC 146 , 2019(3)J.L.J.R.67, 2020(1)MhLj795, 2020(1)MPLJ316, 2019(3)PLJR67, 2019(2)RCR(Civil)321, 2019(3)RLW2070(SC), 2019(3)SCALE864, (2019)5SCC341, 2019 (3) SCJ 75, MANU/SC/0288/2019

No. of pages in Original Judgement: 6

Case Note:

Contract - Liquidated damages - Section 70 of the Indian Contract Act, 1872 - Appeal was against impugned order allowing principal amount of Rs. 84,74,087 in favour of Petitioner, payment of interest at rate of 9% was directed - Whether Appellant was justified in adjusting amount from dues payable to Respondent by deduction from bills raised by Respondent.

Brief Facts of the case:

Present appeal arose out of a dispute under Telecom Regulatory Authority of India Act, 1997. Relief sought through a petition before Telecom Disputes Settlement and Appellate Tribunal, New Delhi ["TDSAT"] by Respondent, Tata Communication Ltd. against Appellant, Mahanagar Telephone Nigam Ltd., was for a recovery of a sum of INR 1,10,57,268 plus interest thereon. TDSAT, on considering Purchase Order, held that, Petitioner was required to provide last mile connectivity as per paragraph 4(iv) of P.O. within two months. Petitioner did not provide required connectivity not only by December 2008 but even by time when it chose to terminate contract on 11th January, 2011. Petitioner's case appeared to be weak and unacceptable in so far as it put blame totally upon Respondent for its inability or failure to provide last mile connectivity. There was some delay by Respondents at initial stage but that alone could not justify or absolve Petitioner's total failure. Further, in absence of any reliable materials as to actual costs which Petitioner had saved by non-compliance with requirements of paragraph 4(iv) of P.O., at best Respondents could have invoked Clause 16 and more particularly, Clause 16.2 which provided for liquidated damages in certain eventualities like failure to deliver stores/services or to install and commission project in whole or in part. Admitted default on part of Petitioner could safely be treated as failure or delay affecting installation/ commissioning of a part of project requiring last mile connectivity. In such a case, as per Clause 16.2(b) of Agreement (P.O.), liquidated damages could be levied on affected part of project. As per Clause 16.2(c), liquidated damages must be limited to a maximum of 12%. In present case, full amount billed and receivable by Petitioner for services rendered was disclosed as Rs. 2,15,25,512, hence, on account of limitation of 12%, Respondents could not have levied and deducted an amount more than Rs. 25,83,181. Instead of adopting this lawful course, Respondents proceeded to unilaterally impose rentals at their own rate of dark fibre. Such action of Respondents amounted to adjudicating a claim in its own favour without any authority for such unilateral act either under Section 70 of Contract Act or under any of provisions of Contract (P.O.). Claim of Petitioner was allowed but in part only. Principal amount which Respondent must refund or pay back to Petitioner would be Rs. 84,74,087. Interest @ 18% could not be allowed in absence of any such stipulation in Agreement (P.O.). Hence, while allowing principal amount of Rs. 84,74,087 in favour of Petitioner, payment of interest at rate of 9% was directed from date amounts became due upto date of this judgment/order.

Held,

In the present case, clauses 16.2 to 16.4 are relevant, and are set out as under:

16.2 (a) <u>FOR DELIVERY OF STORES:</u>

Should the supplier fail to deliver the store/services or any consignment thereof within the period prescribed for delivery, the purchaser shall be entitled to recover 0.5% of the value of the delayed supply for each week of delay or part thereof for a period up to 10 (TEN) weeks and thereafter at the rate of 0.7% of the value of the delayed supply for each week of delay or part thereof for another TEN weeks of delay. In the case of package supply where the delayed portion of the supply materially hampers installation and commissioning of the systems, L/D charges shall be levied as above on the total value of the concerned package of the Purchase Order. However, when supply is made within 21 days of QA clearance in the extended delivery period, the consignee may accept the stores and in such cases the LD shall be levied upto the date of QA clearance.

16.2 (b)<u>FOR INSTALLATION & COMMISSIONING</u>

Should the supplier fail to install and commission the project within the stipulated time the purchaser shall be entitled to recover 0.5% of the value of the purchase order for each week of delay or part thereof for a period upto 10 (TEN) weeks and thereafter @ 0.7% of the value of purchase order for each week of delay or part thereof for another 10 (TEN) weeks of delay. In cases, where the delay affects installation/commissioning of part of the project and part of the equipment is already in commercial use, then in such cases, LD shall be levied on the affected part of the project.

16.2 (c). The Liquidated Damages, as per Clause 16.2 (a) and 16.2 (b) above shall be limited to a maximum of 12%, even in case the DP extension is given beyond 20 weeks.

16.3. Provisions contained in Clause 16.2(a) shall not be applicable for durations (periods) which attract L.D. against Clause 16.2(b) above.

16.4. Quantum of liquidated damages assessed and levied by the purchaser shall be final and not challengeable by the supplier.

13. As has been correctly held by the impugned judgment, a maximum of 12% can be levied as liquidated damages under the contract, which sum would amount to a sum of INR 25 lakh. Since this Clause governs the relations between the parties, obviously, a higher figure, contractually speaking, cannot be awarded as liquidated damages, which are to be considered as final and not challengeable by the supplier. This being the

case, the Appellant can claim only this sum. Anything claimed above this sum would have to be refunded to the Respondent.

In this view of the matter, we uphold the impugned judgment of the TDSAT and dismiss the present appeal.

NINE

Bharti Airtel Ltd. and Ors. Vs. Union of India (UOI) and Ors., 2015

Hon'ble Judges/Coram: Jasti Chelameswar and R.K. Agrawal, JJ.

Relevant Section:

Indian Contract Act, 1872 - Section 11(1)(a) Telecom Regulatory Authority of India Act, 1997 - Section 2, Section 3, Section 3(1), Section 3(2), Section 11, Section 11(1), Section 18; Indian Telegraph Act, 1885 - Section 3(1)(AA), Section 4, Section 4(1); Indian Wireless Telegraphy Act, 1933; - Section 23; Electricity (Supply) Act, 1948 [Repealed] - Section 51, Electricity (Supply) Act, 1948 [Repealed] - Section 59; Telecom Regulatory Authority of India (Amendment) Act, 2000; Constitution of India - Article 14, Constitution of India - Article 32

Equivalent Citation: 2015(4)ABR600, AIR2015SC2583, 2015 (4) CCC 173 , (2015)3CompLJ342(SC), (2015)4MLJ340(SC), 2015(6)SCALE479, (2015)12SCC1, MANU/SC/0613/2015

No. of pages in Original Judgement: 13

Case Note:

Media and Communication - Telegraph service - Extension of license - Section 4 of Indian Telegraph Act, 1885 and Indian Wireless Telegraphy Act, 1933 - Impugned order dismissed Licensees-Appellant's Petition seeking extension of license pertaining to telegraph services - Hence, present appeals - Whether minor variations in language employed by Licensor made any difference in context of right of Licensees to seek extension of licence - Held, license granted under Section 4(1) of Act, 1885 was contract between Licensor and License - Language of clauses of licences indicated that Licensees had no automatic right of renewal/extension on expiry of original tenure of license - Under contract neither Licensor nor Licensee had right to insist that other party should continue with contract - Licensor had discretion to stipulate terms and conditions which were regulated by certain constitutional mandates - Licensees were not compelled to pay any specific tariffs fixed by Licensor, for availing right to use spectrum - Appeals dismissed

Brief Facts of the case:

These five civil appeals Under Section 18 of the Telecom Regulatory Authority of India Act, 1997 (hereinafter referred to as the "TRAI Act") and three writ petitions raise common questions. Each of the Appellants or the Petitioners, as the case may be, in these matters (hereinafter collectively referred to as 'LICENSEES') is a licensee holding a licence granted Under Section 4 of the Indian Telegraph Act, 1885 for providing TELEGRAPH services in the various earmarked service areas.

2. It appears from the judgment of this Court in ***Centre for Public Interest Litigation and Ors.*** *v.* ***Union of India and Ors.*** (2012) 3 SCC 1, hereinafter referred to as ***2G*** case, that the first telegraph link in India was experimented in 1839 between Calcutta and Diamond Harbor separated by a distance of 21 miles. By an act of the British Parliament, known as the Indian Telegraph Act, 1885, the privilege of "establishing, maintaining and working of telegraphs" within the territory of British India was exclusively conferred Under Section 4 upon the Central Government - an expression which bore different meanings at different points of time in this country, the details of which may not be necessary for the purpose of this case. However, proviso to the said section enabled the Central Government to licence any person to exercise the privilege which is otherwise exclusive to the Central Government.

Held,

In the case in hand, the LICENSEES are not compelled to pay any specific tariffs fixed by the LICENSOR (Union of India), for availing the right to use the spectrum. If the price for securing allocation of spectrum is likely to go up because of the procedure of auctioning to have access to spectrum, it goes up because of the market forces. Because there are people who are willing to acquire such a right paying a higher price on the assessment that they would be able to carry on the business profitably even after paying higher amounts for acquisition of spectrum. The LICENSEES are corporate houses with enormous economic power, which enables them to secure adequate expert advice in the matter of financial planning. We cannot believe that they would make any investment without making a reasonable assessment of the possible return on such investment. There is no compulsion by the State in this regard. Therefore, in our view, the reliance placed on the ***Kerala State Electricity Board*** (supra) is wholly untenable.

83. Reliance is placed on the observations made in the ***Special Reference*** (supra) in paragraphs 82 and 146 in support of the submissions of the LICENSEES that auction is not the only method of disposal of natural resources. In our opinion, the LICENSEES' reliance on these paragraphs is wholly misconceived. These two paragraphs, instead of supporting the case of the LICENSEES, are destructive of their contention.

Further, the final conclusions summarized in paragraph 102 of the judgment (SCC) in ***2G*** case make no mention about auction being the only permissible and intra vires method for disposal of natural resources; the findings **are limited to the case of spectrum**. In case the Court had actually enunciated, as a proposition of law, that auction is the only permissible method or mode for alienation/allotment of natural resources, the same would have found a mention in the summary at the end of the judgment.

To summarize in the context of the present Reference, it needs to be emphasized that this Court cannot conduct a comparative study of the various methods of distribution of natural resources and suggest the most efficacious mode, if there is one universal efficacious method in the first place. It **respects the mandate and wisdom of the executive for such matters.** The methodology pertaining to disposal of natural resources is clearly an economic policy. It entails intricate economic choices and the Court lacks the necessary expertise to make them. As has been repeatedly said, it cannot, and shall not, be the endeavour of this Court to evaluate the efficacy of auction vis-à-vis other methods of disposal of natural resources. The Court cannot mandate one method to be followed in all facts and circumstances. Therefore, auction, an economic choice of disposal of natural resources, is not a constitutional mandate. We may, however, hasten to add that the Court can test the legality and constitutionality of these methods. When questioned, the Courts are entitled to analyse the legal validity of different means of distribution and give a constitutional answer as to which methods are 135 Page 136 ultra vires and intra vires the provisions of the Constitution. Nevertheless, it cannot and will not compare which policy is fairer than the other, but, if a policy or law is patently unfair to the extent that it falls foul of the fairness requirement of Article 14 of the Constitution, the Court would not hesitate in striking it down.

(Emphasis supplied)

In para 82, this Court was categoric that the findings of ***2G*** case were limited to the case of spectrum. Similarly, in para 146, this Court observed that this Court "respects the mandate and wisdom of the executive" in the matter of choosing the most suitable method of distribution of natural resources. This Court noted that this is clearly a matter of an economic policy entailing an intricate economic choice and the Court lacks necessary expertise to make such choice. In the light of the observation in para 82 that at least in the matter of disposal of spectrum, auction is the only "permissible and intra vires method for disposal". Therefore, the submission of the LICENSEES is required to be rejected.

For all the above-mentioned reasons, we see no merit in these appeals and writ petitions. Therefore, all the appeals and writ petitions are dismissed. There shall be no order as to costs.

ÞÞÞ

TEN

CITADEL FINE PHARMACEUTICALS AND ORS. VS. RAMANIYAM REAL ESTATES P. LTD. AND ORS., 2011

Hon'ble Judges/Coram: G.S. Singhvi and A.K. Ganguly, JJ.

Acts/Rules/Orders:

Indian Contract Act, 1872 - Section 55; Specific Relief Act 1963 - Section 9

Equivalent Citation: AIR2011SC3351, 2011 5 AWC4861SC, (SCSuppl)2011(5)CHN200, 2011(6)CTC112, JT2011(9)SC265, (2012)1MLJ476(SC), 2011(4)RCR(Civil)894, 2011(8)SCALE301, MANU/SC/0939/2011

No. of pages in the Original Judgement: 8

Case Note:

Contract - Specific performance - Section 55 of Indian Contract Act, 1872;Section 9 of Specific Relief Act, 1963 - Appeal against judgment of High Court holding that Respondents could be given relief of specific performance only to extent of 47 cents of lands that were not part of proceedings under Tamil Nadu Urban Land (Ceiling and Regulations) Act, 1978 - Whether in agreement time was of essence of contract - Held,having regard to previous correspondence and terms of contract time was of essence of contract - Case related to a contract in commercial transaction - Court could take judicial notice of fact that in city of Chennai price of real estate was constantly escalating and clear intention of parties was to treat time as essence of contract - Stipulation as time being of essence of contract was specifically mentioned in Clause 10 and consequences of non-completion were mentioned in Clause 9 - Plaintiff had not discharged its burden within time specified and was not entitled to a specific performance of contract - Suppression of fact that Plaintiff refused to accept cheque sent to it by Defendant in terms of Clause 9 of contract was a material fact - Therefore, Plaintiff/Purchaser was not entitled to any relief in its suit of specific performance - SLP (C) No. 28251/2008 allowed - SLP (C) No. 31269/2008 dismissed.

Brief Facts of the case:

These appeals have been preferred from the judgment and final order dated 2nd September, 2008 passed in O.S.A. No. 332/2007 and C.M.P. No. 1/2007 by the Division Bench of the Madras High Court.

The controversy arose out of a suit of specific performance. M/s. Citadel Fine Pharmaceuticals (Defendant No. 1), a partnership firm, owned 66 cents of agricultural land (hereinafter 'the suit property'), forming a part of total of 2.87 acres of agricultural land in survey Nos. 363, 364, 366/1 of Velachery village, Mamblam, Guindy Taluk, Registration District of Madras, and entered into an agreement for sale of the suit property (hereinafter 'the agreement') for a consideration of Rs. 1,00,00,000/- with M/s. Ramaniyam Real Estates Private Limited (Plaintiff), which was a company incorporated under the Companies Act, 1956 and engaged in the business of constructing buildings.

Held,

his Court has also taken the same view in the case of **Arunima Baruah** v. **Union of India and Ors.** reported in MANU/SC/7366/2007 : (2007) 6 SCC 120. At paragraph 12, page 125 of the report, this Court held that it is trite law that to enable the court to refuse to exercise its discretionary jurisdiction suppression must be of a material fact. This Court, of course, held what is a material fact, suppression whereof would disentitle the suitor to obtain a discretionary relief, would depend upon the facts and circumstances of each case. However, by way of guidance this Court held that material fact would mean that fact which is material for the purpose of determination of the lis.Following the aforesaid tests, this Court is of the opinion that the suppression of the fact that the Plaintiff refused to accept the cheque of Rs.

10 lac sent to it by the Defendant under registered post with A.D. in terms of Clause 9 of the Contract is a material fact. So on that ground the Plaintiff-purchaser is not entitled to any relief in its suit of specific performance.

For the reasons aforesaid, this Court allows the appeal filed by M/s. Citadel Fine Pharmaceuticals (SLP (C) No. 28251/2008) and dismisses the appeal filed by the M/s Ramaniyam Real Estates P. Ltd. (SLP (C) No. 31269/ 2008).

The Court directs M/s. Citadel Fine Pharmaceuticals to return the amount of Rs. 10,00,000/- by an account payee cheque to M/s. Ramaniyam Real Estates P. Ltd., if not already returned, within 4 weeks from date. In default M/s. Citadel Fine Pharmaceuticals will have to pay interest at the rate of 12% per annum on the same from the expiry of the period of 4 weeks from date till actual payment.

Having regard to the facts and circumstances of this case there will be no order as to costs.

ELEVEN

20TH CENTURY FINANCE CORPN. LTD. AND ORS. VS. STATE OF MAHARASHTRA, 2000

Hon'ble Judges/Coram: S.P. Bharucha, V.N. Khare, D.P. Mohapatra, B.N. Kirpal and S.S.M. Quadri, JJ.

Acts/Rules/Orders:

Indian Contract Act, 1872 - Section 148, Section 149 Central Sales Tax Act, 1956 - Section 14, Section 15, Section 2(g), Section 3, Section 4, Section 5, Constitution Of India - Article 226, Article 246, Article 266, Article 269, Article 269(1)(g), Article 269(3), Article 280(1), Article 286, Article 286(1), Article 286(1)(a), Article 286(2), Article 32, Article 366, Article 366(29-A), Article 366(29A)(d); ; Karnataka Sales Tax Act, 1957 - Section 2(t); Tamil Nadu General Sales Tax Act, 1959 - Section 2(n), Tamil Nadu General Sales Tax Act, 1959 - Section 3(A)

Equivalent Citation: AIR2000SC2436, (2000) 30 APSTJ 241, 2000(102(3))BOMLR442, JT2000(7)SC177, 2000(5)SCALE13, (2000)6SCC12, [2000]Supp1SCR120, [2000]119STC182(SC), MANU/SC/0412/2000

No. of pages in the Original Judgement: 21

Case Note:

Constitution - Imposition of Tax - Article 366(29A)(d) of Constitution of India - Petitioner challenge validity of provisions relating to imposition of tax on transfer of right to use goods contained in sales tax laws of States

- High Court was of view that transaction of transfer of right to use goods was species of bailment and transfer was completed only upon delivery of goods - Therefore, situs of sale created by Explanation to Section 2(10) of Maharashtra Act was valid - Hence, this Appeal - Whether, state could levy sales tax on transfer of right to use goods merely on basis that goods put to use were located within its State - Held, State in exercise of power under Entry 54 of List II read with Article 366(29A)(d) were not competent to levy sales tax on transfer of right to use goods which was deemed sale - Appropriate legislature by creating legal fiction could fix situs of sale - Situs of sale would be place where contract was executed and not where goods were located for use - Transaction of transfer of right to use goods could not be termed as contract of bailment as it was deemed sale within meaning of legal fiction engrafted in Article 366(29A)(d) of Constitution - Therefore, location or delivery of goods within State could not be made basis for levy of tax on sales of goods - Legislation of State purported to fix situs of sale in that State could not tax deemed sale which was completed in another State and it could not create taxable event - High Court proceeded on footing that transfer of right to use was different from sale or deemed sale - Petition disposed of.

Ratio Decidendi: ***"State cannot impose tax on sale, which was completed in another State, and create taxable event."***

Brief Facts of the case:

Despite the decisions of this Court in Builders' Association of India v. Union of India MANU/SC/0085/1989 : [1989]2SCR320 and Gannon Dunkerley & Co. v. State of Rajasthan MANU/SC/0437/1993 : (1993)1SCC364 , the controversy as regards the power of the State legislature to levy sales tax under Clause (29A)(d) of Article 366 of the Constitution in the context of the question where is the taxable event on the transfer of right to use any goods remained unresolved. In this group of cases, we are concerned with the power of States legislature to levy sales tax on the transfer of right to use any goods envisaged under Clause (29A)(d) of Article 366 of the Constitution on the premise that goods put to use are located within their States, Several States by their legislations have levied tax on the transactions of transfer of right to use goods on the location of goods at the time of their use within their States irrespective of the place where the agreement for such transfer of the right to use such goods is made. The questions therefore, that arise for consideration in these cases are, whether a State can levy sales tax on transfer of right to use goods merely on the basis that the goods put to use are located within its State irrespective of the facts that - (a) the contract of transfer of right to use has been executed outside the 4 State; (b) sale has taken place in the course of an inter-State trade; and (c) sales are in the course of export or import into the territory of India. The appellants' case is that, the State legislature cannot so frame its law as to convert an outside sale or a sale in the course of import or a sale in the course of an inter-State trade or commerce into a sale inside the State,

The appellants in civil appeals and the petitioners in the writ petitions filed under Article 32 of the Constitution and transferred petition, and respondent in Civil Appeal Nos. 6218-23/95 are the companies incorporated under the Companies Act and some have their registered offices at places outside the respondent States and others have inside the States. They carry on business of leasing diverse equipments. According to them, they entered into Master Lease Agreements with the lessee i.e. the party who desired to take equipment for use on hire. The appellants and the petitioners agree to give on lease diverse machinery/ equipments listed in the Lease Summary Schedule, subject to terms and conditions stipulated in the Master Lease Agreements. The Lease Summary Schedule only mentions the broad category of equipment proposed to be leased and the correct value thereof. The Master Lease Agreement provides that orders for individual equipment will be placed by the appellants at the instance of lessees and that the equipment to be leased will be dispatched by the manufacturer or supplier concerned to the locations specified in the lease. Thereafter, at the instance of the lessees, the appellants place their purchase orders to the suppliers or manufacturers for supply of individual items or equipments falling within the category and correct value mentioned in the Master Lease Agreement Schedules. The appellants' and the petitioners' further case is that, they disburse the value of equipment to the suppliers and at the instance of the appellants and thc pctitioners the suppliers deliver the equipments to the lessees at the specified locations for use. After the equipments are delivered and put to use, the lessee executes supplementary lease schedules acknowledging due receipt of the lease equipments, and such supplementary lease deeds form an integral) part of the Master Lease Agreement, Such is the nature of business carried on by the appellants and the petitioners in this group of cases. According to the appellants and the petitioners, one transaction of transfer of right to use goods is subjected to sales tax by more than one States. On such a transaction, some States levy tax on the appellants and the petitioners, merely because the goods were found to be located in their States at the time of execution of contract which has taken place outside the State. Some States levy tax when the goods are delivered in their States for use in pursuance of agreements of transfer executed outside their States and some States tax such transactions of deemed sales on the premise that agreements for transfer of right to use have been executed within their States, The appellants and the petitioners, therefore, have challenged the validity of the legislations by various States whereby one transaction of transfer of right to use goods has been subjected to tax by more than one States.

Held,

In the light of the above discussion, as the equipment involved was unspecified goods and indeed an order for purchase of an unspecified equipment was made by the respondent after the lease, the respondent did not become owner of the equipment till the same was despatched to the hirer so the transaction under Sub-clause (d) could be complete only after the completion of the sale of the equipment which happened only when the equipment was actually delivered to the hirer in Hyderabad (Andhra Pradesh). Therefore, the transaction of deemed sale under Sub-clause (d) cannot be said to be complete on the execution of the contract of master lease. If that be so, the question of the deemed sale being an Inter-State sale would not arise. On this aspect, the Andhra Pradesh High Court has referred to the view of the Bombay High Court in 20th Century Finance Corporation 1989 (75) STC 217 and differed from the same. But the Andhra Pradesh High Court failed to take note of the fact that though the deemed sale is subject to the same limitations as the sale, in view of the provisions of Article 286 of the Constitution and the provisions of Sections 3 and 4 of the Central Sales Tax Act, and the State is denuded of the power to tax an inter-State transaction, yet in this case there has been no inter-State deemed sale. The fact that the master lease agreement refers to hiring of the equipment and the fact that at the instance of the hirer the appellant placed the order for purchase are immaterial. There is always a difference between purchasing any goods for the reason that hirer wanted to hire it and the hirer himself ordering purchase of the goods. In the Instance case, the purchase of the equipment was by the respondent, the fact that the hirer wanted to hire the equipment might have prompted the respondent to place an order for its purchase but that fact is irrelevant in arriving at the conclusion whether the lease in respect of non-existent unspecified equipment would be complete on the execution of the master lease. On this aspect, we have held that before an unspecified equipment reaches the hirer, the sale of the equipment by the respondent itself would not be complete. The deemed sale under Sub-clause (d) is only a consequential transaction which follows the completion of the sale in favour of the respondent and cannot precede it.

The transaction in question, namely, entering into master lease between the hirer and the respondent and placing the order for purchase of an equipment desired to be taken on lease by the hirer as an order for purchase of an equipment at the instance of the hirer is an attempt to save sales tax either on sale of the equipment or on the deemed sale. The Revenue can have no grudge against a person who so arranges his affairs as to minimise his tax liability under the provisions of a taxing statute. Indeed, it is expected of the Revenue to ensure that correct tax as ordained by the Statute is paid by every assessable person-no more no less. But that does not mean the tax evasion should be equated with tax planning. The tax evasion has to be dealt with promptly under the provisions of the relevant taxing statute. It appears to us that clubbing of the two transactions-the master lease and the purchase of the equipment pursuant thereto purporting to be at the instance of the hirer with instructions to the manufacturer/supplier to deliver the same to the hirer, to wit, as if the transaction under Sub-clause (d) is also an inter-State transaction whereas the sale alone will be an inter-State transaction - cannot but be an attempt to evade the tax leviable on transaction under Sub-clause (d) of Clause (29-A) of Article 366 of the Constitution.

The civil appeals, writ petitions and transferred case are disposed of accordingly as indicated above.

Before parting, we wish to record our thanks to Mr. C. S. Vaidyanathan, the learned Additional Solicitor-General who so readily assisted the Court as amicus curiae.

TWELVE

THE TRUSTEES OF THE PORT OF MADRAS VS. K.P.V. SHEIK MOHAMED ROWTHER & CO. AND ORS., 1962

Hon'ble Judges/Coram: A.K. Sarkar, J.L. Kapur, M. Hidayatullah, Raghubar Dayal and S.K. Das, JJ.

Acts/Rules/Orders:

Constitution Of India - Article 226; Indian Contract Act, 1872 - Section 148, Section 151, Section 152, Section 161

Equivalent Citation: [1963]Supp2SCR915, MANU/SC/0051/1962

No. of pages in the Original Judgement: 10

Case Note:

Commercial - rates - Sections 148, 151, 152 and 161 of Indian Contract Act, 1872 - appeal filed against decision of High Court to forbear appellants from imposing scale 'E' rates upon respondents - scale 'E' rates imposed on master, owner or agent of vessel to be paid in respect labour of port trust rendered idle on account of some lapse on part of ship owners - respondent challenged imposition on ground that liability of steam owners end at time when they handed over goods on port - they were not liable to pay rates for labour sitting idle on port - Supreme Court observed that liability of owners of ships ends only when goods delivered to consignee and not when goods handed over on port - labour employed on port to render service to vessels - they sits idle due to fault of owners of vessel without any default of their own - held, rates rightly imposed.

Brief Facts of the case:

The appellants, the Trustees of the Port of Madras, hereinafter called the Board, appeal against the order of the High Court of Madras allowing the writ petitions filed under Art. 226 of the Constitution by each of the respondents and issuing a writ of mandamus directing the appellants to forbear from enforcing the scale 'E' rates of the Madras Port Trust Scale of Rates and from requiring the signing of the Shore Labour Requisition Form from the steamer agent.

2. The respondents, who are either partnership firms or limited companies, carry on the business of steamer agents at Madras. The Board, with the sanction of the Central Government, made amendments to the Madras Port Trust Scale of Rates in 1958. By the amendment, scale 'E' was added under Chapter V. It was to come into force from March 1, 1958. The scale laid down charges to be paid by masters, owners or agents of vessels in respect of Port Trust labour requisitioned and supplied but not fully or properly utilised. The charges, for the sake of brevity, may be said to be on account of the labour of the Port Trust, Madras, rendered idle on account of some lapse on the part of the ship-owners or on account of extra payment to labour for the simultaneous working of more than one hook at the vessel's hatch. The labour requisition Form to be submitted by the steamer-agents was also modified and the new form contained an undertaking on the part of the steamer-agents for the payment of the charges laid down in the Board's scale of rates from time to time in respect of labour rendered idle or not properly utilised and also for working more than one hook simultaneously at the hatch. These amendments in the scale of rates were made by the Board in the exercise of its power under s. 42 of the Madras Port Trust Act, 1905 (Mad. Act II of 1905), hereinafter called the Act. This section empowers the Board to frame a scale of rates at which and a statement of the conditions under which any of the services specified in the various clauses of the section shall be performed by the Board or by a person to whom any service has been relinquished under s. 41-A of the Act. Thereafter, the respondents, viz., the streamer-agents, filed petitions under Art. 226 of the Constitution, in the High Court of Madras, and prayed for the issue of a writ of mandamus directing the Board not to enforce these rates and not to require the filling in of the new form. They contended that (1) the ship-

owners and the steamer-agents cannot be made liable for charges for shore labour employed in the receiving or removal of cargo and such charges must be borne by the consignee; (II) s. 39 of the Act provided for the performance of services by the Board and the other sections provided for the imposition and recovery of rates for the services performed for the vessel and services performed for the goods. Services in the former category are to be paid for on behalf of the carrier i.e., by the master, ship-owner or the steamer-agent, and the services in the latter category constitute a liability on the consignee; (iii) the Board has power to impose and recover rates only for services rendered and that they have no right to impose charges by way of compensation for default or to collect charges from masters, owners or agents of vessels in respect of operations not properly falling under the head of discharge of cargo from the vessel; (iv) prior to 1914, the steamer-agents acted as landing-agents for removing cargo from ship to pier and collected for these services from the consignees a separate charge known as 'landing charge' in addition to the freight. When the quays were constructed and cargo came to be landed there, the Board took over the landing of goods and collected quay dues instead of 'landing charges' which were wholly paid by the consignees. These quay dues later on merged in the 'harbour dues' collected by the Board from the consignees; (v) usually, the steamer agent informs the Traffic Manager the probable date of arrival of the vessel under his agency, tonnage hatch-wise of cargo to be landed at Madras and the number of hatches proposed to be worked. Under the revised procedure adopted by the Board on August 1, 1957, before a ship has reached its berth, the steamer agent is required to make an application and a deposit in his current account to cover charges for the working of the vessel in respect of overtime, supply of cranes, water and appliances and from March 1, 1958, to meet the scale 'E' contingencies also; (vi) the operation which goes on at the quay is described thus : After the Port Trust pilot brings the vessel to the berth allotted to her :

Held,

We do not agree with the contention that the charges for labour rendered idle are in the nature of compensation or damages in respect of any loss, inconvenience or expenses caused to the Board or its shore-labour in consequence of any default attributed to the master of the ship. There is no question of damages. The labour has been engaged. It is paid for the time during which it remains idle, for no fault of its own. Charges for that are levied from the person who required that labour and is responsible for its remaining idle. Of course, if the idle time was due to the default of the labour, no such charges are required to be paid by the ship-owner.

We are therefore of opinion that the impugned charges were rightly levied by scale 'E' on the master, owner or agent of the vessels and that the Board could insist on the steamer-agent requisitioning the shore-labour to express an undertaking in the form for requisitioning labour that he will pay the charge laid down in the Board's scale of rates from time to time in respect of labour rendered idle or not properly utilised and also for working more than one hook simultaneously at a vessel's hatch.

We therefore allow the appeals with costs here and the Courts below, set aside the order of the Court below and dismiss the writ petitions. There will be one hearing fee.

Appeals allowed.

THIRTEEN

A. Lakshmanaswami Mudaliar and Ors. Vs. Life Insurance Corporation of India and Ors., 1962

Hon'ble Judges/Coram: B.P. Sinha, C.J., J.C. Shah, K.C. Das Gupta, K.N. Wanchoo and P.B. Gajendragadkar, JJ.

Relevant Section:

INDIAN CONTRACT ACT, 1872 - Section 2

Equivalent Citation:

AIR1963SC1185, [1963]33CompCas420(SC), (1963)1CompLJ248(SC), (1963)1CompLJ248(SC), [1963]Supp2SCR887, MANU/SC/0062/1962

No. of pages in the Original Judgement: 5

Case Note:

Company - ultra vires resolution - Section 2 of Indian Contract Act, 1872 - resolution passed in extraordinary general meeting of company to form trust - appellants were authorised to pay amount of Rs. 200000 to trust - Life Insurance Act brought into force and all assets and liabilities of company transferred to respondent - respondent claimed refund of amount entrusted to trust - Supreme Court observed that resolution denoting funds of company was not within objects mentioned in memorandum of association and was ultra vires - appellants were responsible for passing resolution as office bearers of company - held, appellants were personally liable to make good the amount belonging to company.

Brief Facts of the case:

This is an appeal from the order dated December 20, 1958, of the Life Insurance Tribunal in case No. 21/XV of 1958.

The United India Life Assurance Company Ltd. - hereinafter called 'the Company' - incorporated under the Indian Companies Act, 1882, with the principal object of carrying on life insurance business in all its branches was registered as an insurer under the Life Insurance Act, VI of 1938 for carrying on life insurance business in India. On July 15, 1955, at an extraordinary General Meeting of the shareholders of the Company, the following resolution, amongst others, was passed :-

"Resolved that a donation of Rs. 2 lakhs be sanctioned from out of the Shareholders' Dividend Account to the M.Ct.M. Chindambaram Chettyar Memorial Trust proposed to be formed with the object, inter alia, of promoting technical or business knowledge, including knowledge in insurance.

Resolved further that the Directors be and are hereby authorised to pay the aforesaid sum to the Trustees of the aforesaid Trust when it is formed."

Held,

Where a Company does an act which is ultra vires, no legal relationship or effect ensues therefrom. Such an act is absolutely void and cannot be ratified even if all the shareholders agree. Re. Birkback Permanent Benefit Building Society [1912] 2 Ch. 183. The payment made pursuant to the resolution was therefore unauthorised and the trustees acquired no right to the amount paid by the Directors to the trust.

The only question which remains to be considered is whether the appellants were personally liable to refund the amount paid to them. Appellants 2 and 4 were at the material time Directors of the Company and they took part in the meeting held under the Chairmanship of the fourth appellant in which the resolution, which we have held ultra vires, was passed. As office bearers of the Company who were responsible for passing the resolution ultra vires the Company, they will be personally liable to make good the amount belonging to the Company which was unlawfully disbursed in pursuance of the resolution. Again by s. 15 of the Life Insurance Corporation Act, 1956 the Life Insurance Corporation is entitled to demand that any amount paid over to any person without consideration, and not reasonably necessary for the purposes of the controlled business of the insurer be ordered to be refunded, and by sub-section (2) authority is conferred upon the Tribunal to make such order against any of the parties to the application as it thinks just having regard to the extend to which those parties were respectively responsible for the transaction or benefited from it and all the circumstances of the case. The trustees as representing the trust have benefited from the payment. The amount was, it is common ground, not disposed of before the Corporation demanded it from the appellants, and if with notice of the infirmity in the resolution, the trustees proceeded to deal with the fund to which the trust was not legitimately entitled, in our judgment, it would be open to the Tribunal to direct the trustees personally to repay the amount received by them and to which they were not lawfully entitled.

The appeal therefore fails and is dismissed with costs.

Appeal dismissed.

FOURTEEN

Construction & Design Services Vs. Delhi Development Authority, 2015

Hon'ble Judges/Coram: T.S. Thakur and Adarsh Kumar Goel, JJ.

Acts/Rules/Orders:

Indian Contract Act, 1872 - Section 73, Section 74

Equivalent Citation: 2015(1)CDR153(SC), MANU/SC/0313/2015

No. of pages in the Original Judgement: 6

Case Note:

Contract - Compensation - Indian Contract Act, 1872 - Respondent awarded contract to Appellant for constructing sewerage pumping station - Contract contained compensation clause for delay - Appellant failed to complete contract - Compensation imposed by Respondent - Court held compensation in nature of penalty and basis for compensation not revealed - Overturned by High Court on appeal - When and to what extent can the stipulated damages for breach of a contract be held to be in the nature of penalty in absence of evidence of actual loss - To what extent can the stipulation be taken to be the measure of compensation for the loss suffered even in absence of specific evidence - Whether the burden of proving the amount stipulated as damages for breach of contract was penalty is on the person committing the breach - Whether the High Court was correct in upholding the compensation imposed by the Respondent

The Respondent awarded a contract to the Appellant for constructing a sewerage pumping station. The contract contained the following clause: 'In the event of the contractor failing to comply with this condition, he shall be liable to pay as compensation an amount equal to one percent or such smaller amount as the Superintending Engineer Delhi Development Authority (whose decision shall be final) may decide on the said estimated cost of the whole work for everyday that the due quantity of work remains incomplete'.

The Appellant failed to complete construction and the contract was terminated. The Superintending Engineer of the Respondent levied compensation of Rs. 20,86,446/- for delay in execution of the project. The High Court dismissed the suit of the Respondent for payment of compensation, holding that the Respondent had not treated the time fixed for performance of the contract as of essence and the compensation stipulated in the agreement was in the nature of penalty. The basis for levy of compensation had not been indicated so as to determine whether the compensation claimed was reasonable. On appeal, the High Court reversed the previous decision. Hence, the present Appeal.

Held,

Take for illustration construction of a road or a bridge. If there is delay in completing the construction of road or bridge within the stipulated [pic]time, then it would be difficult to prove how much loss is suffered by the society/State. Similarly, in the present case, delay took place in deployment of rigs and on that basis actual production of gas from platform B-121 had to be changed. It is undoubtedly true that the witness has stated that redeployment plan was made keeping in mind several constraints including shortage of casing pipes. The Arbitral Tribunal, therefore, took into consideration the aforesaid statement volunteered by the witness that shortage of casing pipes was only one of the several reasons and not the only reason which led to change in deployment of plan or redeployment of rigs Trident II platform B-121. In our view, in such a contract, it would be difficult to prove exact loss or damage which the parties suffer because of the breach thereof. In such a situation, if the parties have preestimated such loss after clear understanding, it would be totally unjustified to arrive at the conclusion that the party who has committed breach of the contract is not liable to pay compensation. It would be against the specific provisions of Sections 73 and 74 of the Indian Contract Act. There was nothing on record that compensation contemplated by the parties was in any way unreasonable. It has been specifically mentioned that it was an agreed genuine pre-estimate of damages duly agreed by the parties. It was also mentioned that the liquidated damages are not by way of penalty. It was also provided in the contract that such damages are to be recovered by the purchaser from the bills for payment of the cost of material submitted by the contractor. No evidence is led by the claimant to establish that the stipulated condition was by way of penalty or the compensation contemplated was, in any way, unreasonable. There was no reason for the Tribunal not to rely upon the clear and unambiguous terms of agreement stipulating pre-estimate damages because of delay in supply of goods. Further, while extending the time for delivery of the goods, the Respondent was informed that it would be required to pay stipulated damages."

17. Applying the above principle to the present case, it could certainly be presumed that delay in executing the work resulted in loss for which the Respondent was entitled to reasonable compensation. Evidence of precise amount of loss may not be possible but in absence of any evidence by the party committing breach that no loss was suffered by the party complaining of breach, the Court has to proceed on guess work as to the quantum of compensation to be allowed in the given circumstances. Since the Respondent also could have led evidence to show the extent of higher amount paid for the work got done or produce any other specific material but it did not do so, we are of the view that it will be fair to award half of the amount claimed as reasonable compensation.

Accordingly, this appeal is partly allowed and the decree granted by the High Court is modified to the effect that the Respondent-Plaintiff is entitled to half of the amount claimed with rate of interest as awarded by the High Court. Out of the amount deposited in this Court, the Respondent will be entitled to withdraw the said decretal amount and the Appellant will be entitled to take back the remaining. The appeals are disposed of accordingly.

FIFTEEN

National Textile Corporation (Gujarat) Ltd. Vs. State Bank of India and Ors., 2006

Hon'ble Judges/Coram: S.B. Sinha and P.P. Naolekar, JJ.

Relevant Section:

INDIAN CONTRACT ACT, 1872 - Section 60; Section 61, Section 59

Equivalent Citation: AIR2006SC2927, AIR2006SC2927, [2006]134CompCas164(SC), (2006)6CompLJ448(SC), (2006)6CompLJ448(SC), JT2006(7)SC285, 2006(4)RCR(Civil)124, 2006(7)SCALE627, (2006)7SCC542, [2006]Supp(4)SCR411, MANU/SC/8404/2006

No. of pages in the Original Judgement: 11

Case Note:

Company - advancement of loans - Section 18(1) of Industries (Development & Regulation) Act, 1951 and Section 2 (f) and Schedule to Sick Textile Undertakings (Nationalization) Act, 1974 and Indian Contract Act, 1872 - appeals against Order holding that in light of precedents loans advanced by petitioner bank prior to 14.2.1969 guaranteed by Authorized Controller and by State Government, guarantee for post-take-over period would fall under category No. 1 (a) of Second Schedule and it would not fall in category No. 4 of part B - contention that High Court erred in holding that loan was advanced during post-takeover period during which management was with corporation and facility was given by bank to continue to avail credit facilities to pay amount of loan on renewal - further contention that undertaking given by Controller for continuing to obtain said facilities would not make outstanding dues on account of priority claim of company and there exists difference between loan and liability whereas principal amount would come within purview of priority claim, claim of interest would not - textile undertakings were sick ones - managements of such mills were taken over for purpose of revival - if in that process Authorized Controller was required to raise loan either from bank or from financial institution other than bank or from any other person or availed any other credit, same would come within purview of Category-I liability being post-takeover management period - such loan would not be renewal of pre-takeover loan - Section 2(f) requires that there should be instrument in writing by which obligor obliges himself to pay past liability and instrument should bear interest - admittedly no such document admitting and acknowledging past loan and fresh document was executed - liability of owner continues even during take-over period - it would not mean that any act done by statutory authority or State would be binding on owner - Gujarat Financial Corporation or State of Gujarat having furnished guarantee on their own behalf, same indisputably would continue to remain binding on them - such guarantees which were furnished by Gujarat Financial Corporation or State of Gujarat would be enforceable against them - High Court not justified in taking views which it did - impugned Orders set aside with liberty to parties to file appropriate suits or proceedings before appropriate forum for recovery of remaining amount, provided any cause of action therefore survives - appeals allowed.

Brief Facts of the case:

These appeals involving identical questions of law and fact were taken up for hearing together and are being disposed of by this common judgment. The factual matrix of the matter, however, would be noticed from Civil Appeal No. 2316 of 2000.

The management of the New Manekchowk Spinning and Weaving Mills Company Limited was taken over in terms of Section 18(1) of the Industries (Development & Regulation) Act, 1951. The Gujarat State Textile Corporation Limited was appointed as its Authorized Controller. The period of takeover was extended upto 31.03.1974. The Parliament thereafter enacted the Sick Textile Undertakings (Nationalization) Act, 1974, (for short, 'the Act') which came into force with effect from 01.04.1974 in terms whereof the right, title and interest of the said textile mills vested absolutely in the Central Government. The Central Government, however, issued an appropriate notification whereby and whereunder the said mills instead of continuing to vest in the Central Government were directed to vest in the National Textile Corporation (Gujarat).

Held,

The following principles relevant to the present case emerge from the aforesaid discussion: (1) An arbitration clause is a collateral term of a contract as distinguished from its substantive terms; but nonetheless it is an integral part of it; (2) however comprehensive the terms of an arbitration clause may be, the existence of the contract is a necessary condition for its operation; it perishes with the contract; (3) the contract may be non est in the sense that it never came legally into existence or it was void ab initio; (4) though the contract was validly executed, the parties may put an end to it as if it had never existed and substitute a new contract for it solely governing their rights and liabilities thereunder; (5) in the former case, if the original contract has no legal existence, the arbitration clause also cannot operate, for along with the original contract, it is also void; in the latter case, as the original contract is extinguished by the substituted one, the arbitration clause of the original contract perishes with it; and (6) between the two falls many categories of disputes in connection with a contract, such as the question of repudiation, frustration, breach etc. In those cases it is the performance of the contract that has come to an end, but the contract is still in existence for certain purposes in respect of disputes arising under it or in connection with it. As the contract subsists for certain purposes, the arbitration clause operates in respect of these purposes.

The said decision would apply in the instant case.

In Lalit Mohan Pandey v. Pooran Singh and Ors.MANU/SC/0422/2004 : AIR2004SC2303 , whereupon also the learned Counsel placed reliance, this Court emphasized the need to construe the statute having in mind the object underlying the same by stating the principle of purposive construction. Thus, the remedies available to the Bank under the Indian Contract Act would continue to remain available to the respondent-Bank even if the 1958 Act applies.

For the reasons aforementioned, we are of the opinion that the High Court was not correct in taking the views, it did. The judgments and orders passed by the High Court are, therefore, set aside with liberty to the parties to file appropriate suits or proceedings before appropriate forum(s) for recovery of the remaining amount, provided any cause of action therefore survives. Subject to the observations made herein, the appeals are allowed. No costs.

SIXTEEN

CITI BANK N.A. AND ORS. VS. STANDARD CHARTERED BANK AND ORS., 1995

Hon'ble Judges/Coram: R.C. Lahoti and Ashok Bhan, JJ.

Acts/Rules/Orders:

Indian Contract Act, 1872 - Section 41, Section 61, Section 62, Section 63; Constitution Of India - Article 142; Indian Evidence Act, 1872 - Section 114

Equivalent Citation: AIR2003SC4630, I(2004)BC211(SC), I(2004)BC211(SC), [2003]57CLA24(SC), [2003]117CompCas554(SC), (2004)1CompLJ121(SC), (2004)1CompLJ121(SC), 2004(2)CTC374, JT2003(10)SC597, 2003(8)SCALE364, (2004)1SCC12, [2003]47SCL582(SC), [2003]Supp4SCR489, 2004(1)UJ537, MANU/SC/0793/2003

No. of pages in the Original Judgement: 16

Case Note:

Commercial - Banking - Special Courts (Trial of Offences Relating to Transactions in Securities) Act, 1992 - Indian Contract Act - Sections 41, 62 and 63 - Onus upon the plaintiff to show that debt was still subsisting which the plaintiff had failed to discharge by producing any evidence - Production of the document by the defendant from his custody raised a rebuttal presumption of the discharge of the debt - Novatio, rescission or alteration of a contract can only be done with the agreement of both the parties of a contract - Both the parties have to agree to substitute the original contract with a new contract or rescind or alter and cannot be done unilaterally - Where an instrument, a cheque or negotiable instrument, is given by the debtor and accepted by the creditor, the question whether the instrument was taken as an absolute payment or a conditional payment is one of the fact depending on the intention of the parties - Citi Bank becomes entitled to restitution of the total amount paid by it to Standard Chartered Bank (principal and interest) along with interest @ 12% p.a. from the date of receipt of payment by SCB provided it is paid on or before 30th November, 2003 and in default to pay the interest @ 15% p.a. from the date of receipt of payment till it is repaid by the Standard Chartered Bank - Citi Bank would also be entitled to receive back the amount of costs it had paid to Standard Chartered Bank under the decree of the Special Court but the same would not carry any interest

Brief facts of the case:

This judgment shall dispose of Civil Appeal No. 7941 of 1995 arising in Suit No. 22 of 1994 (filed by Standard Chartered Bank against Citi Bank & Others) decided on 10th July, 1995 and Civil Appeal No. 8340 of 1995 arising in Suit No. 20 of 1994 (filed by Citi Bank against Standard Chartered Bank & Others), decided on 7th July, 1995. Suits were tried by the Special Judge appointed under the Special Courts (Trial of Offences Relating to Transactions in Securities) Act, 1992, hereinafter referred to as 'the Act'.

2. During 1991-92, Reserve Bank of India noticed that large scale irregularities and mal practices were committed in transactions in both the Government and other securities, by some brokers in collusion with the employees of various banks and financial institutions. The said irregularities and mal practices led to the diversion of funds from banks and financial institutions to the individual accounts of certain brokers. To deal with this situation and, in particular, to ensure speedy recovery of the huge amount involved and to punish the guilty and restore confidence in and maintain the basic integrity and credibility of the banks and financial institutions, this Act was enacted for establishment of Special Courts to be presided over by a sitting Judge of the High Court to be nominated by the Chief Justice of the High Court within the local limits of whose jurisdiction the Special Court is situated, with the concurrence of the Chief Justice of India. The Act provided for appointment of one or more Custodian for attaching the properties of the offenders with a view to prevent diversion of such property by the offenders. The Custodian, on being satisfied, on information received that any person has been involved in any offence

relating to transactions in securities after the 1st day of April, 1991 and on and before 6th June , 1992 could notify the name of such person in the Official Gazette. Special Courts were given the jurisdiction to deal with cases of civil as well as criminal liability of the notified person.

Held,

This appeal has been filed by the CMF against the decree passed against it in Suit No. 20 of 1994. In Civil Appeal No. 7941 of 1995 we have recorded a finding that Suit No. 20 of 1994 filed by the Citi Bank was a back to back suit to save itself in case a decree was passed against it in the suit filed by the Standard Chartered Bank in Suit No. 22 of 1994. In other words, it was a contingent suit based on the result in Suit No. 22 of 1994. Mr. Kapadia, learned senior counsel appearing for the CMF had addressed arguments at length supporting the submissions made on behalf of Citi Bank against the Standard Chartered Bank. He did not say much against the decree passed in favour of the Citi Bank. We need not deal with the contentions raised by Mr. Kapadia as we have accepted the Civil Appeal No. 7941 of 1995 and set aside the decree passed against the Citi Bank in Suit No. 22 of 1994. The consequence of the acceptance of the said appeal would be that this appeal has to be accepted which arises from a contingent suit. Accordingly, the appeal filed by the CMF is accepted and the decree passed against it in Suit No. 20 of 1994 is set aside and the suit is ordered to be dismissed with costs throughout.

As a consequence to the aforesaid CMF becomes entitle to restitution of the total amount paid by it to the Citi Bank (principal and interest) along with interest @ 12% p.a. from the date of payment provided it is paid on or before 5th December, 2003 and in default to pay the interest @ 15% p.a. from the date of payment till it is repaid by the Citi Bank. Though the appellant had prayed for interest @ 20% p.a.(which had been awarded by the Special Court) but we have reduced the same keeping in view that interest rates have come down substantially in the recent years. In Civil Appeal No. 7941 of 1995 also we have granted interest @ 12% p.a. only.

The CMF would be entitled to receive the amount of costs it had paid under the decree of the Special Court but without interest. Costs in this appeal are assessed at Rs. 20 lakhs. CMF would be entitled to the costs before the Special Court of the equivalent amount which were awarded against it by the Special Court while decreeing the suit against it.

Both the appeals stand allowed in the aforesaid terms.

SEVENTEEN

TRUSTEES OF THE PORT OF BOMBAY VS. PREMIER AUTOMOBILES LTD.. 1980

Hon'ble Judges/Coram: D.A. Desai and P.N. Shinghal, JJ.

Relevant Section:

INDIAN CONTRACT ACT, 1872 - Section 152

Equivalent Citation: AIR1981SC1982, 1981(83)BOMLR28, (1981)1SCC228, [1981]1SCR532, MANU/SC/0099/1980

No. of pages in the Original Judgement: 8

Case Note:

Bombay Port Trust Act (Bom VI of 1879) Sections 61B, 87 - True Scope and effect of-Expression 'subject to the other provisions of this Act' in Section 61B--Expression whether excludes Section 87--Bailment--Nature of-Non-contractual bailment-Effect-Board if liable for wrongs by its employees appointed under Act-Tort-Indian Contract Act (IX of 1872), Sections 151, 152, 161.

When the plaintiffs in a suit for damages against the Port Trust plead that the 'Board' constituted under Section 4 of the Bombay Port Trust Act, 1879, moved their consignment in their capacity as bailees thereof, there is no contractual bailment according to pleadings of the parties or on the wording of Section 61B of the Bombay Port Trust Act; but the responsibility of the Board is as bailees of the consignment and the claim is no other than by way of an action in tort. There is no justification for the view that the plaintiffs base their claim on the breach of a mere statutory duty of the Board under Section 61B of the Bombay Port Trust Act.

A bailment is not technically and essentially subject to the limitations of an agreement, and the notion of privity need not be introduced in an area where it is unnecessary, for bailment, arises out of possession, and essentially connotes the relationship between a person and the thing in his charge. It is sufficient if that possession is within the knowledge of the person concerned. It follows that a bailment may very well exist without the creation of a contract between the parities and it essentially gives rise to remedies which, in truth and substance, cannot be said to be contractual. Speaking simply and generally the law of torts is concerned with those situations where the conduct of one party causes or threatens harm to the interests of the other party. As a duty is cast on the Board under Section 61A to take charge of the goods immediately upon landing, the Legislature took care to 4lav down and define the nature and the extent of that liability, which was set out, in terms to be that of a bailee. A non-contractual bailment is predominantly a tortious relation.

Brief Facts of the case:

This appeal by certificate is directed against the judgment of the Bombay High Court dated July 17, 1970, by which it upheld the judgment of the trial court dated March 3, 1965, decreeing the suit of the plaintiffs-respondents for Rs. 35,000 and interest with a part of their costs. It so happened that although there was initially much controversy about the facts the parties realised the futility of disputing some glaring facts and agreed to take a decision, even in the trial court, on what they once described as "interim consent terms", but to which they have stuck all through. We shall refer to them in a while, after stating some of the facts on which both the trial and the appellate courts have placed reliance. That will bring out the significance of the "consent terms" and make them more intelligible.

The Premier Automobiles Ltd, hereinafter referred to as the plaintiffs, imported 13 cases of machinery from Italy. Case No. 249, which is the subject-matter of the controversy before us, contained an internal grinding machine weighing over 3 tonnes. It arrived in Bombay on February 21, 1960, by S.S. Jalsilton Hall. The "Board", constituted under Section 4 of the Bombay Port Trust Act, 1879. for short the Act, was a body corporate with a perpetual succession and a common seal. It was called "the Trustees of the Port of Bombay" and could sue and be sued by that name. We shall, however, refer to it as "the Board" for that is how it has been referred to in the Act and the impugned judgment. Since" the Board was charged with the duty of carrying out the provisions of the Act, and had, in particular, the duty, under Section 61A(1) of the Act, to take charge immediately upon the landing of any goods, it took charge of case No. 249 also on its landing in Bombay on February 21, 1960. The Board has in fact filed document Ex. K to prove that the case was in a damaged condition when it landed on February 21, 1960, and that attention to that fact was drawn of the handling agents M/s. Scindia Steam Navigation Co. Ltd. It purports to be a contemporaneous document. The case was placed on a four-wheeler trolly and was being carried to one of the sheds in the docks when it fell down and the machine contained in it was severely damaged. Several employees of the Board were in charge of the case and the trolly at that time.

Held,

The High Court has observed that any other view would "virtually render the provisions of Section 61B largely nugatory". But the very next sentence gives out the reason for that view, for the High Court has gone on to observe that that would be so if paragraph 2 of Section 87 is construed otherwise, namely, that "for any and every misfeasance, malfeasance or non-feasance of its employee, the Board is given complete immunity." That, however, is not what Section 61B and paragraph 2 of Section 87 provide for, as we have pointed out earlier, only a very few of the Board's employees are appointed under the Act and all that the paragraph provides is that the Board shall not be responsible for any misfeasance, malfeasance or nonfeasance on the part of only those employees. They may, for aught one knows, be responsible personally for what they do, but it is not a correct proposition of law to say that the view which has found favour with us would virtually render the provisions of Section 61B "largely nugatory".

In the view we have taken, it is not necessary for so to examine the validity of the bye-laws to which reference has been made by the High Court. They were produced before us towards the close of the hearing, for the arguments proceeded and were based on the true meaning and construction of Sections 61B and 87 (paragraph 2) and it was agreed that our decision thereon would govern the fate of this case. We should not therefore be taken to have expressed any opinion about the validity of the bye-laws in question. It will be sufficient for us to say that the decision here or below will not be conclusive of their validity or invalidity for purposes of the present case or like controversy.

In the result, the appeal succeeds and is allowed. The judgment and decree of the High Court are set aside and the suit is dismissed. In the circumstances of the case, the parties shall pay and bear their own costs throughout.

ÞÞÞ

EIGHTEEN

Radhakrishna Sivadutta Rai and Ors. Vs. Tayeballi Dawoodbhai, 1961

Hon'ble Judges/Coram: B.P. Sinha, C.J., P.B. Gajendragadkar and Raghubar Dayal, JJ.

Relevant Section:

INDIAN CONTRACT ACT, 1872 - SECTION 230; SECTION 236

Equivalent Citation: AIR1962SC538, [1962]Supp1SCR81, **MANU/SC/0054/1961**

No. of pages in the Original Judgement: 8

Case Note:

The suit for damages for breach of contract - Does Brokers buying and selling of notes if and when constitutes terms of 'contract' - Validity of contract as per commercial usage - The contract on behalf of disclosed partner and maintainability of the suit as per act - Indian Contract Act 1872 S.230.

Brief facts of the case:

This appeal by a certificate granted by the Calcutta High Court arises out of a suit filed by the three appellants against the respondent to recover Rs. 83,640/-. The three appellants are respectively the Firm Radhakishan Shivdutt Rai which carries on business at Banaras and Ramkumar Lal for himself and as karta of his joint family as well as Madan Gopal for himself and as karta of his joint family, the latter two being the partner in the first-mentioned Firm Radhakrishna Sivadutta Rai; for convenience we will refer to the partnership firm hereafter as the appellant. The respondent Tayeballi Dawoodbhai is a partnership firm which carries on business at Calcutta. The appellant's case was that the appellant and the respondent had entered into a contract in the first instance on December 18, 1950, through brokers named T.N. Mehrotra & Co., Calcutta. This contract was later confirmed by two letters written respectively on January 3 and 15, 1951, by the appellant to the respondent and replied to by the respondent. By this contract the respondent agreed to sell 1000 bales of Banaras Hemp particulars of which were set out in the plaint. According to the appellant, by a letter written on March 14, 1951, the appellant in part performance of the said contract accepted delivery of 110 bales of Banaras Hemp No. 1 and 50 bales of Banaras Hemp No. 2; this delivery was made by the respondent to L.N. Poddar & Co., who acted as the agent of the appellant and paid the price of the said 160 bales. In this transaction the respondent realised Rs. 3,840 from the said L.N. Poddar & Co. in excess of the actual price of the goods delivered to the said company. Inspite of the repeated demands made by the appellant the respondent failed to deliver the balance of the goods contracted for and thus committed breach of the contract. That is how the appellant claimed Rs. 79,800 as difference between the market rate on March 31, 1951, and the contract rate of the balance deliverable under the contract in suit. This amount was claimed as damages for the breach of contract. In addition an amount of Rs. 3,840 was claimed as having been paid in excess of the value of 160 bales delivered to L.N. Poddar & Co., on behalf of the appellant.

Held,

What then would be the effect of the relevant recitals in the letter on which Mr. Pathak relies? In this connection it is necessary to recall that we are reading these letters along with the bought and sold notes, and that the bought and sold notes have unequivocally and clearly indicated that the appellant was acting on behalf and on account of the disclosed principal Khaitan & Sons. If we read the letters in the light of the bought and sold notes it would be clear that the signature of the appellant will not have much significance, nor would the use of the word "we" by the appellant or "you" by the respondent make any difference. Parties knew that the appellant was acting on behalf of the disclosed principal. It is not suggested that in such a case every time the agent has to sign expressly stating that he is acting on behalf of the disclosed principal. Therefore, if the appellant was acting for the disclosed principal the fact that he did not add the relevant description to his signature, or used the word "we" in the operative portion of the letter would not materially alter the fact spoken to by the notes that the appellant was acting on behalf of the disclosed principal. It cannot be suggested that these letters intended to alter the position disclosed by the notes. The letters, like the confirmation slips, are, and must be, presumed to be consistent with the notes; and so it would be unreasonable to attach undue importance to the signature and to the use of the relevant words "we" and "you" on which reliance has been placed. In our opinion, therefore, the Appellate Court was right in holding that even if the bought and sold notes are read along with the confirmation slips and the two letters of January 3, 1951, and January 15, 1951, the conclusion is inescapable that the appellant entered into the contract on behalf of the disclosed principal Khaitan & Sons Ltd. If that be so, it follows as a matter of law that the appellant is not entitled to bring the present suit.

Mr. Pathak faintly attempted to argue in the alternative that even if the appellant was acting on behalf of the disclosed principal it would be entitled to sue because from the subsequent conduct of the parties a contract to the contrary could be reasonably inferred. We have, however, not allowed Mr. Pathak to argue this point. It was conceded by the appellant before the Appellate Court that if it was held that the plaintiff firm was acting as agent for Khaitan & Sons Ltd., the suit was not maintainable. This concession was made in view of the provisions of s. 236 of the Contract Act. Besides, the alternative plea which Mr. Pathak wanted to raise does not appear to have been expressly pleaded or considered in the trial court.

In the result the appeal fails and is dismissed. In the circumstances of this case we direct that the parties should bear their own costs in this Court.

Appeal dismissed

NINETEEN

UNION OF INDIA (UOI) AND ORS. VS. R.P. YADAV, 2000

Hon'ble Judges/Coram: K.T. Thomas, D.P. Mohapatra and Ruma Pal, JJ.

Acts/Rules/Orders:

Constitution Of India - Article 14, Article 226; Indian Contract Act, 1872 - Section 18, Section 18(1), Section 19, Section 20, Section 21, Section 22, Section 23, Section 24, Section 25, Section 26, Section 27, Section 28, Section 29, Section 30, Navy Act, 1957 - Section 11, Section 11(2), Section 14(1), Section 15, Section 16, Section 16(a), Section 16(b), Section 17, Section 18, Section 184, Section 184(1), Section 3(20), Section 41

Equivalent Citation: AIR2000SC2252, JT2000(6)SC371, 2000LabIC2366, 2000(3)LLN492(SC), 2000(4)SCALE600, (2000)5SCC325, (2000)SCC(LS)681, [2000]Supp1SCR196, 2000(2)SCT1049(SC), 2001(1)SLJ148(SC), 2001(1)SLJ154(SC), 2000(4)SLR591(SC), (2000)3UPLBEC2174, MANU/SC/0391/2000

No. of pages in the Original Judgement: 8

Case Note:

Contract - consent - whether artificer apprentice of Indian Navy who had been given re-engagement for certain period after obtaining his consent for it entitled to withdraw consent and demand his release from force as of right - members of defence services including Navy have privilege of being entrusted with tasks of security of Nation - it is privilege which comes way of only selected persons who succeeded in entering service and maintained high standard of efficiency - persons who in opinion of prescribed authority not permanently fit for any form of naval service may be terminated and discharged from service - sailor entitled to seek discharge from service at end of period for which he has been engaged and this right subject to exceptions provided in Regulations - such provisions rule out concept of any right in sailor to claim as of right release during subsistence of period of engagement or re-engagement - such measure required in larger interest of country - question answered in negative.

Brief Facts of the case:

The question that arises for determination in these appeals is whether an Artificer Apprentice of Indian Navy who has been given a re-engagement for a certain period after obtaining his consent for it is entitled to withdraw the consent and demand his release from the force as of right? Another question which also arises is what bearing the decision of this Court in Anuj Kumar Dey v. Union of India MANU/SC/1006/1997 : (1997)1SCC366 on the above question.

In the appeal arising from SLP (C) No. 9839 of 1999, the respondent R. P. Yadav has already been released from the force in compliance with the direction of the Delhi High Court in the impugned judgment. Indeed in the Order dated 14-2-2000, this Court recorded the submission of Mr. Soli J Sorabjee, learned Attorney General for India, that so far as the respondent R. P. Yadav is concerned, the Union of India is only interested in having the question of law decided and even if it is decided in favour of the Union of India, they will not deny the benefit which R.P. Yadav has claimed in this petition. The period of re-engagement granted in the case of R. P. Yadav has also expired. But in the case of Raj Kumar, the respondent in the appeal arising from SLP (C) No. 16848 of 1999, the period of re-engagement granted to the said respondent is due to expire on 31st January, 2002. Therefore, it will be convenient to refer to the relevant facts in the case of Raj Kumar that is the civil appeal arising from SLP (C) No. 16848 of 1999.

Held,

The refusal of the appellants was arbitrary and violative of Article 14 of the Constitution because the appellants have released others whose cases were similar to Raj Kumar's. R. P. Yadav who had been re-engaged to serve till 31st January, 2000 was released on 31st January 1999. Our attention was also drawn by Raj Kumar's counsel to the case of one Azad Singh Ruhil. Azad Singh had also approached the High Court for his release under Article 226. This was directed by the learned single Judge on 28th January, 1999. No appeal was preferred by the appellants from this order and Ruhil was released. The appellants have submitted a 'note' after the arguments were concluded and judgment reserved, to the effect that since Ruhil had not signed the contract of re-engagement as Raj Kumar had, they had decided not to prefer an appeal. The reasoning is specious particularly in view of the stand taken by the appellants in their counter affidavit before the High Court viz., that once the offer made for re-engagement by the sailor was accepted by the appellants the contract was complete and could not be rescinded.

I would, for all these reasons dismiss the appeals and, as far as Raj Kumar is concerned, with costs. I regard that by expressing my opinion in favour of dismissal of the appeals, I am differing with the views expressed by my learned Brothers. But I do so with respect and despite the impassioned submissions made by the learned Additional Solicitor General on behalf of the Government that the defence of the country would be jeopardised by a possible sudden efflux of trained personnel. Apart from the fact that this was not the ground stated by the appellants in the order of rejection, to accept this as a ground for allowing the appeal, in the view that I have taken, would be to decide the case not according to law but on policy. And, speaking for myself, I would rather (sic) the country's defence did not rest on unwilling shoulders.

[1. Unwillingness for Re-engagement.

(a) On publication of Expiry of Engagement Serial if a sailor does not wish to reengage for further service a certificate of unwillingness as per Appendix 'D' to this order is obtained from him. A copy of this certificate is to be retained with sailors service documents and another forwarded to the Bureau of Sailors, Bombay.

(b) Requests for signing for further service from sailors who have once expressed unwillingness, are not be entertained under any circumstances, e.g., changed domestic circumstances, loss of prospective employment opportunity etc. as this upsets manpower planning, recruitment and progress of pension papers.

(c) However, sailors who have once expressed their unwillingness to sign an undertaking for further service and subsequently wish to re-engage on promotion, will be considered for re-engagement only if they are willing to sign for a minimum period of two years, provided the request is put up at least nine months prior to the date of release. Short term re-engagements of one to nine months in order to earn pension of the rank will not be granted.]

TWENTY

Tarsem Singh Vs. Sukhminder Singh, 1998

Hon'ble Judges/Coram: Saiyed Saghir Ahmad and M. Jagannadha Rao, JJ.

Relevant Section:

INDIAN CONTRACT ACT, 1872 - SECTION 20; SECTION 65

Equivalent Citation: AIR1998SC1400, 1998(2)ALLMR(SC)528, 1998(2)ARBLR1(SC), 1998 (2) AWC 125 (SC), 1998(2)BLJR819, 1998(100(2))BOMLR512, 1998 (1) CCC 163 , 1998(1)CTC443, JT1998(2)SC149, 1998-2-LW303, (1998)IIIMLJ54(SC), (1998)120(3)PLR802, 1998(2)RCR(Civil)94, 1999(2)RCR(Civil)185, RLW1998(2)SC183, 1998(2)SCALE58, (1998)3SCC471, [1998]1SCR456, MANU/SC/0158/1998

Case Note:

Contract - earnest money - Sections 2, 10, 12, 13, 14, 15, 16, 17, 18, 20, 22, 23, 24, 65, 73 and 74 of Indian Contract Act, 1872 - parties entered into contract for sale of certain land and certain amount was paid to petitioner as earnest money - suit for specific performance filed when petitioner did not execute sale deed and decreed by Trial Court - in appeal Additional District Judge observed that both parties suffered from mistake of fact as to area of land and sale-consideration - decree for specific performance not passed but decree for refund of earnest money passed which was confirmed by High Court - appeal by special leave - petitioner contended according to forfeiture clause in contract respondent not entitled to refund of earnest money - observed that contract was void from its inception as observed by Additional District Judge - forfeiture clause in contract also void - petitioner could not legally forfeit amount and seek enforcement of forfeiture clause - decree for refund of earnest money confirmed.

No. of pages in the Original Judgement: 21

Brief Facts of the case:

The petitioner, who owned 48 Canals 11 marlas of agricultural land in village Panjetha, Tehsil and District Patiala, entered into a contract for sale of that land with the respondent on 20.5.1988 @ Rs. 24,000 per acre. At the time of the execution of the agreement, an amount of Rs. 77,000/- was paid to the petitioner as earnest money. Since the petitioner did not execute the sale deed in favour of the respondent in terms of the agreement although the respondent was ready and willing to perform his part of the contract, the latter, namely, the respondent filed the suit for Specific Performance against the petitioner which was decreed by the trial court. The decree was modified in appeal by the Additional District Judge who was of the opinion that the parties to the agreement, namely, the petitioner and respondent both suffered from a mistake of fact as to the area of the land which was proposed to be sold as also the price (sale-consideration) whether it was to be paid at the rate of per "Bigha" or per "Canal". The Lower Appellate Court also found that the respondent was not ready and willing to perform his part of the contract. Consequently, the decree for Specific Performance was not passed but a decree for refund of the earnest money of Rs. 77,000 was passed against the petitioner. This was upheld by the High Court.

Held,

This case before the Privy Council also related to sale of certain villages for which some money had been paid in advance. The sale was found to be inoperative as there was a misapprehension as to the rights of the transferor in the villages which he purported to sell and that the true nature of those rights was discovered much later. In this background, the Privy Council held the agreement to have been "discovered to be void". The Privy Council, therefore, passed a decree for compensation in favour of the vendee and in assessing that compensation, the sum of money, which was advanced, was included in the amount of compensation decreed with 6% interest payable from the date of suit.

To the same effect is an old decision of the Calcutta High Court in Ram Chandra Misra & Ors V. Ganesh Chandra Gangopadhya & Ors, AIR (1917) Cal 786, in which it was held that an agreement entered into under a mistake and misapprehension as to the relative and respective rights of the parties thereto is liable to be set aside as having proceeded upon a common mistake.

In this case, there was an agreement for lease of the mogoli brahmatter rights of the defendants in certain plots of land. Both the parties were under the impression that the brahmatter rights carried with them the mineral rights. It was subsequently discovered that brahmatter rights did not carry mineral rights. The High Court held that the agreement became void under Section 20 of the Contract Act as soon as the mistake was discovered and, therefore, the plaintiffs were entitled to refund of money advanced under a contract which was subsequently discovered to be void.

We may point out that there are many facets of this question, as for example (and there are many more examples), the agreement being void for any of the reasons set out in Section 23 and 24, in which case even the refund of the amount already paid under that agreement may not be ordered. But, as pointed out above, we are dealing only with a matter in which one party had received an advantage under an agreement which was "discovered to be void" on account of Section 20 of the Act. It is to this limited extent that we say that, on the principle contained in Section 65 of the Act, the petitioner having received Rs. 77,000 as earnest money from the respondent in pursuance of that agreement, is bound to refund the said amount to the respondent. A decree for refund of this amount was, therefore, rightly passed by the Lower Appellate Court.

For the reasons stated above, we see no force in this Special Leave Petition which is dismissed.

PPP

Videos & Tv Shows On Law & Exim

List of some important videos & TV shows on Law & EXIM by Adv. Jayprakash Somani on his YouTube Channel 'Jayprakash Somani EXIM & Legal'

Legal Videos: Hindi -English

1) SLP in Supreme Court / Special Leave Petitions in the Supreme Court of India

2) Transfer of Civil & Criminal Cases by the Supreme Court of India / Transfer of Matrimonial Cases

3) Appellate Jurisdiction of the Supreme Court of India

4) Jurisdictions of the Supreme Court of India

5) Public Interest Litigation in the Supreme Court of India / PIL in Supreme Court

6) Article 32 Writ Petitions in the Supreme Court of India

7) Bail Matters Top 10 Supreme Court Cases

8) FIR Quashing in High Court & Supreme Court

9) Bail & Anticipatory Bail Matters in Supreme Court

10) Insolvency & Bankruptcy Matters in the Supreme Court

11) Insolvency & Bankruptcy Code 2016 Part 1

12) Insolvency & Bankruptcy Code 2016 Part 2

13) Insolvency & Bankruptcy Code 2016 Part 3

14) Corporate Liquidation Process

15) Supreme Court Rules & Procedures Webinar of 2.5 hour on Zoom

16) RDDBFI Act, 1993 (Introduction)

17) The Indian Contact Act 1872

18) Negotiable Instruments Act (Introduction)

19) How to avoid matrimonial disputes& some more videos

20)SEBI Matters in the Supreme Court

21) Matrimonial Matters: Supreme Court's 20 Case Laws

22) Consumer Matters Supreme Court's 20 Case Laws

23) Service Matters Supreme Court's 20 Case Laws

24) How to Search Lawyer for Your Matter

25) Property Matters Supreme Court's 20 Case Laws

26) Bail Matters: Supreme Court's 20 Case Laws

27) Supreme Court / High Court Vacation Benches

28)69000 Teacher's Recruitment Matters of UP Government in the Supreme Court

29) Contempt of Court Matters in the Supreme Court

30) Advocate Act's Matters in the Supreme Court

31) Business Law Matters in the Supreme Court

32) Banking Matters in the Supreme Court

33) Labour Law Matters in the Supreme Court

34) Arbitration Matters in the Supreme Court

35) Careers in Law -Zoom Webinar by Adv. Jayprakash Somani

36) Civil Matters in the Supreme Court

37) Consumer Protection Act | Consumer Matters in the Supreme Court

38) Corporate Matters in the Supreme Court

39) Criminal Matters in the Supreme Court

40) Role of Respondent in the Supreme Court of India

41) Motor Vehicle Accident Matters in Supreme Court with case laws

42) Article 131 Original Suits in Supreme Court

43)PIL in Supreme Court/ Public Interest Litigations in the Supreme Court of India'

44)CAB Citizenship Amendment Bill is not Unconstitutional

45) Supreme Court of India Cases & Process – Marathi

46) Legal Services Export / Export of Legal Services

47) Transfer of Matrimonial Cases by the Supreme Court of India

48) Public Interest Litigation PIL

49) The Specific Relief Act (Introduction)

50) Corporate Insolvency Resolution Process CIRP

51)ABMM's Career 5 - Careers in Law

52) Transfer of cases by Supreme Court

53) Writ Petitions in High Court & Supreme Court of India

54) Supreme Court Jurisdictions - Appeals, SLP, Writ Petitions, Transfer, Original, Review, Curative

55)LEGAL INDIA TV Show: Cases Handled in Supreme Court

56) Corporate Liquidation Process

57) Legal Services Export / Export of Legal Services

EXIM Videos: Hindi -English

1) Yes, I can do Import Export Business Easily! 36 points excellent video in Hindi

2) Yes, I can do Import Export Business Easily! 36 points excellent video in English

3) Import Export Business – Hindi video

4) Import Export Business - English video

5) Export Import Marathi TV Interview

6) Scope for Commerce Students in International Business- TV Show

7) Scope for Management Student in International Business- TV Show

8) Scope for Engineering Students in International Business – TV Show

9) Women in International Business- TV Show

10) How to do Import Export Business Successfully!'

11) Where one can get full information on Import Export Business?

12) What to do import & export?

13) Import Export Workshop/ Training/Course/ Diploma

14) How to Start Import Export Business & How to grow it. Live Webinar

15) Success Stories & Failure Stories in Import & Export Business

16) For MSME Scope in Export & Import...

17) Exports In Agri. & Food Products – English & some more videos

18) Exports to Dubai, Aabudhabii. e. UAE

19) Jewellery Exports from India

20) How to attend EXIM workshop to become excellent Exporter

21) Import Export Best Training Course – Online & Offline

22) Agri Product Export

23) Scope for Woman in International Business

24) Management Graduates Scope in International Business

25) Pharma Product's Export

26) Best Import Export Course | Practical Training | Aaronica Global Exim

27) Import Export Business for Commerce Graduates

28) How Do I Get Export Orders? Finding International Buyers

29) What Is APEDA In Import Export Business?

30) Which Is The Best Product To Export From India?

31)EXIM Remark by Manoj Kumar Faridabad

32)EXIM Remarks by Mahesh Telangana

33) What Licenses I Need To Start Import/ Export?

34) How Can I Increase My Import Export Business?

35) Which Is Best B2B Website For Import/Export Business?

36) Export Import Management with Global Marketing

37) How to Start Export Import Business | 51 Points Video

38) Scope for Commerce & Other Graduates in International Business
39)BE A SUCCESSFUL EXPORTER FOR OUR NATION - Marathi video
40) Export of Textile , Cotton, Agri., Food, & other products & services
41) Exports from MP, CG, MH, GJ & CA in Fresh Fruits & Vegetables
42) Exports in Agri. & Food Products- Hindi
43) Start your Online/E-Commerce Business
44) How to Start Export Import Business & Grow it
45) Exports in Textile & Other Products
46) Start and grow EXIM business - Live English Webinar
47)'Import Export Business!' Why, Who, What & How can one do it easily!!
48) Live: Export of Product & Services During & After Lock Down Period
49) Frauds in Import Export Business
50) Import Export for Business Man
51) Import & Export for Women
51) Import & Export for Graduate & Post - Graduate Students
52) Agriculture Exports from India
53) Digital Marketing Setup - Marathi
54)2nd Secret of Successful Businessman
55) Digital Marketing Set up
56) Legal Services Export / Export of Legal Services
57) Export & Import with UAE
58) Service Exports / Exports by Service Providers
59) Import Export Workshop/ Training/Course/ Diploma
60) Exports & Imports with USA
61) Selection on Product for Export
62) Top Products Exported from India
63) What to do import & export?
64)ABMM Career 2 - 'Careers in Business & Industries
65) How to do Import Export Business Successfully!'
66)5 Secrets of Successful Businessman
67) Export from MP, Chhattisgarh & Vidarbha Nagpur
68)EXIM Hindi - Textile & Apparel Export
69)EXIM Hindi - Export Import Practical Training In Delhi, Kolkata, Mumbai and Pune
70) Import Export Business
71) Import Export Business Hindi
72) Import Export Business English video

73) Import Export Business Marathi

74) Women in International Business by Exim Guru Adv. Jayprakash Somani

75) Opportunities in Foreign Trade- Adv. Jayprakash Somani's special interview

List Of Adv. Jayprakash Somani's Books

1. Supreme Court of India's Leading Case Laws on 'Insolvency & Bankruptcy Code 2016'
2. Bail Matters – Supreme Court's Latest Leading Case Laws
3. Arbitration Matters- Supreme Court's Latest Leading Case Laws
4. Property Matters - Supreme Court's Latest Leading Case Laws
5. Matrimonial Matters- Supreme Court's Latest Leading Case Laws
6. Election Matters- Supreme Court's Latest Leading Case Laws
7.SEBI Matters- Supreme Court's Latest Leading Case Laws
8. Banking Matters- Supreme Court's Latest Leading Case Laws
9. Service Matters- Supreme Court's Latest Leading Case Laws
10. Contempt of Court Matters- Supreme Court's Latest Leading Case Laws
11. Consumer Protection Matters- Supreme Court's Latest Leading Case Laws
12. Corporate Law- Supreme Court's Latest Leading Case Laws
13. Supreme Court's AOR Exam- Leading Cases
14. Armed Force Tribunal - Supreme Court's Latest Leading Case Laws
15. Acquittal From 376 - Supreme Court's Latest Leading Case Laws
16. Negotiable instrument – Supreme Court's Latest Leading Case Laws
17. Contract Act- Supreme Court's Latest Leading Case Laws
18. Insider trading- Supreme Court's Latest Leading Case Laws
19. Foreign Exchange and Management Act- Supreme Court's Latest Leading Case Laws
20. Income Tax Act- Supreme Court's Latest Leading Case Laws
21. Company Law- Supreme Court's Latest Leading Case Laws
22. Competition & Monopoly Matters- Supreme Court's Latest Leading Case Laws
23. Compassionate Appointment- Service Matters- Supreme Court's Latest Leading Case Laws
24. Compulsory Retirement- Service Matters- Supreme Court's Latest Leading Case Laws
25. Voluntary Retirement- Service Matters- Supreme Court's Latest Leading Case Laws
26. Removal/Dismissal/Termination from Service- Supreme Court's Latest Leading Case Laws

27. Seniority- Service Matter- Supreme Court's Latest Leading Case Laws

28. Promotion- Service Matter- Supreme Court's Latest Leading Case Laws

29. Equal Pay for Equal Work- Service Matter- Supreme Court's Latest Leading Case Laws

30. Condition of Service- Service Matter- Supreme Court's Latest Leading Case Laws

PPP

These Books are available online at

1. **Notion Press:** https://notionpress.com/author/jayprakash_somani
2. **Amazon:** https://www.amazon.in/s?k=jayprakash+somani
3. **Flipkart:** https://www.flipkart.com/search?q=Jayprakash%20Somani

PPP

9 798885 698382

Printed by Libri Plureos GmbH in Hamburg,
Germany